PUTTING OUT

PUTTING OUT

THE ESSENTIAL PUBLISHING RESOURCE
FOR LESBIAN AND GAY WRITERS

EDITED BY EDISOL W. DOTSON
4TH EDITION

CLEIS
PRESS

Published in the United States by Cleis Press
Inc., P.O. Box 14684, San Francisco, California
94114.

Book Cover Design: Scott Idleman
Text Design: Frank Wiedemann
Cleis logo art: Juana Alicia
Printed in the United States
Fourth Edition
10 9 8 7 6 5 4 3 2 1
ISBN:0-939416-86-7
ISBN:0-939416-86-5 (pbk.)
Library of Congress Catalog Card
Number: 94-77798

Acknowledgments

This book would not have been possible without the cooperation of the book publishers, magazines, journals, newspapers, newsletters, theaters,
and agents who took the time to provide me
with the substance of the book.

Also, I am grateful to Patricia Nell Warren,
Scott O'Hara, Susan Chasin, Shannon Turner,
and Gail Leondar-Wright for their contributions
to this edition.

In addition, I am grateful to Felice Newman
and Frédérique Delacoste, and the staff at Cleis
Press for the continued support and belief in this
project. It is always a pleasure to work with
them.

Finally, I would like to thank my friends who
are all a part of this project and who have
supported me and it from the very beginning.
Without my friends, I am nothing and no one.

To Richard Labonté

&

To my father, Edisol Beecher Dotson, who has found the larger life

Disclaimer

The purpose of this guide is to provide a partial listing of those book publishers, magazines and journals, newspapers and newsletters, theaters, and agents who publish or produce or represent material with lesbian and/or gay themes. The information contained in this guide should be used only for general reference and should not be taken as an absolute list of publishers or producers or agents who accept material with lesbian and/or gay themes.

Publication of the name of any individual or organization or company or entity in this guide is not to be construed as any indication of the sexual orientation of such individual or organization or company or entity. And likewise, publication of any company or organization or entity in this guide is not to be construed as any indication of the publishing preference of such company or organization or entity.

All information given in the listings contained in this guide concerning contracts or payments to writers from publishers or producers or agents is given solely as preliminary and general information and is not to be considered legally binding in any way.

This guide is intended to be a resource only. Submitting work to any publisher or company or organization or entity or producer or agent listed in this guide does not guarantee that the writer's work will be published or produced or accepted. Any actual publishing or producing or accepting of any writer's work is done solely at the discretion of that publisher or company or organization or entity or agent to whom the work is submitted. Every effort has been made to ensure the accuracy of the listings that appear in this guide. However, typographical errors as well as other errors in content are possible. The editor and the publisher shall not be held responsible or accountable for any action resulting from the misprint of information in this guide.

In addition, every effort has been made to verify the mailing addresses, phone numbers, e-mail addresses, URLs, and contact names of those listings that were a part of any and all previous editions of this guide and that are a part of this new edition, or any and all of the new listings that are a part of this current edition. However, it is possible that any publication or company or organization or entity or individual has ceased to be in business at the time this new edition has been printed. The editor and the publisher shall not be held responsible or accountable for any mailing that is returned to sender by the United States Postal Service or any other mailing or postal service marked "NO SUCH ADDRESS," or "ADDRESS UNKNOWN," or "RETURN TO SENDER," or any other such marking generally used by the United States Postal Service or any other mailing or postal service.

The publisher and the editor shall assume no responsibility to any person or entity with respect to loss or damage caused or alleged to be caused, directly or indirectly, by the information contained in this guide. Purchase or use of this guide binds the purchaser or user to the terms and conditions set forth above.

Contents

PREFACE

I am a writer. It has taken me a long time to begin to feel comfortable making this statement. I still feel uneasy at times when someone asks me what it is I do; people ask this often and I feel as if they are waiting to hear something great and fantastic. I have often seen disappointment on those questioning faces when I answer.

The danger in answering "I am a writer" are the assumptions or expectations, on the part of the one asking the question, that writing is all I do and is what "makes my living." People seem excited about meeting a writer, as if we (writers) are somehow special. (Well, aren't we?)

The next question is generally, "Have you been published?" This is the question that always unnerves me. The question is asked as if being a writer is dependent on being published. Being published is not what makes a writer a writer. Being published is what makes a writer a published writer. A writer is someone who writes. If you put words on paper, you are a writer. If a person is truly a writer, I believe, she or he will write whether or not they are published.

Not too long ago I came across my report cards from my years in grammar school. In the comments area from a first-grade teacher, she wrote that "Eddie has shown an interest in writing stories." I was shocked when I read this. Mostly because I have no memory of first grade, but also because I had no idea that my interest in being a writer had begun at so early an age.

I have at times doubted my own writing abili-ties, sometimes to the point where I have thought of never writing again. It used to be rejection letters that spawned this doubt. The doubt also came after reading some of my writing and being completely horrified by what I read. I am now immune (mostly) to rejection, but not to my own bad writing. Coming across the first-grade report card is something I think of whenever I feel dejected about my writing. How can I not continue to do something that is obviously what I am meant to do? I know that what I am about to say is a double negative, but I will say it anyway: I cannot *not* write. Perhaps this is true for you, as well. Otherwise, you would not be reading this book.

Many (many, many, many) years have gone by since I showed an interest in writing stories in first grade. And while it is true that I have had a few short stories published, it is also true that I have an unpublished novel (and ideas for at least two more), two unpublished nonfiction manuscripts, dozens of unpublished short stories, and countless pages of unpublished poems. The words keep coming. The fact that they remain on my computer's hard drive or in boxes underneath my desk does not make me something different from a writer. Writing is what defines me, not the fill-in-the-blank jobs I do to survive. They are just jobs and nothing more.

Still, I want to be published, certainly to satisfy my ego, but also because I have a great deal to say and I want the world to hear it all. This is why I continue to edit and to use this

book. This new edition of *Putting Out* has
more than 100 new publishing opportunities
for me, and for you. Though some of the listings in the previous edition no longer exist,
many of them are still here and have been
updated with current mailing addresses, phone
numbers, fax numbers, e-mail addresses, World
Wide Web addresses, and contact names.

In her essay in this book, Shannon Turner
writes, "While popular wisdom might have it
that the truly great writers got where they are
because of their exquisite raw talent, my experience has been that self-confidence and persistence are equally important." I think this is
very sound and valuable advice for any writer.
Just as words keep coming to me, so do rejection letters. But this does not prevent me from
putting out my work.

So, I'll say it again, once more with feeling:
I am a writer.

E. W. D.
April 1997

WILDCAT PRESS: FROM KITTEN TO CAT

by Patricia Nell Warren

Wildcat Press started as an idea in 1991, while I was promoting my fifth novel, *One Is the Sun*. Like many authors, I had discovered that the big contract with the big trade house isn't always what it's cracked up to be. There were issues of royalty payments, and creative control of how my work was packaged. *One Is the Sun* took nine years to write, and when it was published in 1991, Ballantine failed to promote it adequately. So I leaped into the trenches and circumnavigated the U.S. for six months in my Toyota pickup, doing a successful homemade national book tour for *One Is the Sun,* and setting in motion the sales for 30,000 copies of the book.

When the tour was over, I realized that authors can take the initiative in marketing their own work. It was time to stop complaining and start doing.

At first, my idea was a personal imprint for book anthologies of already-published short works, like magazine articles and essays. For instance, I'd written scads of things about cats—why not capitalize on the growing market for cat books? But in 1993, when L.A. publicist Tyler St. Mark took me on as a client, we started thinking bigger—of a full-fledged independent trade publisher that would publish my entire body of work. Tyler and I formed a limited partnership. In 1994 we launched our first title: *Harlan's Race,* best-selling sequel to *The Front Runner.*

Today, despite jarring economic problems in the publishing business, it is definitely the golden age of the independently publishing author. More and more authors become alarmed at agent and publisher mismanagement of their books and start stepping in. With the "emerging gay book market" of the early 1970s now a diverse and dynamic market niche, gay, lesbian, bisexual, and transgender authors have the opportunity to think of their body of work as a long-term business asset. Most of the well-known authors of the 1970s and 1980s—for example, Rita Mae Brown, Armistead Maupin, Edmund White—are still publishing. Anyone who has an ongoing market for their books, however modest the subniche, can continue to keep their works earning for them—as long as they do the right PR and keep their costs within bounds.

As *Harlan's Race* came out, I was already making legal moves to get back the English language and foreign rights to my books, which I had so merrily sold off in the 70s and 80s (that was what authors did then).

Many authors do not realize that a publisher who has failed to publish a book, or who lets a book go out of print, has no legitimate reason not to revert the rights to the author free of charge. They might even sell you the plates if they have them, saving you all those typesetting and make-ready costs. Dial Press and William Morrow willingly reverted the hardcover rights to *The Last Centennial, The Front Runner, The Fancy Dancer,* and *The Beauty Queen.* As I write this, Ballantine has just reverted *One Is the Sun.*

But a subsidiary right that still makes money for a licensee is a different matter. The only

11

way we could get *The Front Runner's* and *The Fancy Dancer's* paperback rights was to bid against Penguin/Plume when the seven-year licenses came up for renewal. This we did, and won. Previously, over fourteen years, both books had sold nonstop for Penguin. We published our first trade paperbacks in 1996, and these titles are now selling nonstop for us. So Wildcat has an instant backlist.

A book's U.S. success can have a ripple effect abroad. *The Front Runner* had been published in a number of editions and translations. Two of these—the Japanese edition and the U.K. edition from Gay Men's Press—were still going strong; others we tracked down and got the rights reverted. This opened the door to Wildcat's obtaining permission to republish the existing translation and market our our own foreign-language editions. We are already in production with our own Spanish edition of *The Front Runner,* titled *El Atleta,* translated by Luis Bauz. Within the year, we will launch on the Spanish-speaking book market in the U.S. and abroad. We already have Japanese and Spanish pages on our web site (http://www.gaywired.com/wildcat).

On the jobber front, we have distributors in Canada (Marginal), Australia (Bulldog Books), and U.K.-Europe (Turnaround). Other beckoning markets: Asia and South Africa, from whence I've had fan mail for years. In Japan, Fusosha brought out *Harlan's Race* in April 1997. In South Africa, despite high custom duties and retail markups, there is a newborn market for lesbian, gay, bisexual, and transgender books because of human rights protections in the new constitution. We are broadening the foreign exposure by donating books to nonprofit organizations and archives in other countries.

I am lucky to have a solid international readership of both gay and straight people who tend to read everything I write. But many

authors who are known mainly in the U.S. have an equally great potential for overseas sales and reader appreciation as well. This is because as the gay rights movement grows in other countries, there is a hunger for books about gay life that cannot always be fed from other nations' existing publishing and literary resources.

For ventures in other media, including stage and film, Wildcat Communications is our non-book arm. Yes, it's true that Paul Newman optioned *The Front Runner.* But he didn't pick up the option. The rights were actually bought by Frank Perry in 1977, and passed through several hands afterward; I am now in litigation to get them back. Conventional wisdom says that authors can't get film rights back, but I'm going to try. Public interest in a movie version of *The Front Runner* is still intense. My suggestions to any author who wants to go independent can also work for most any small press. Here are some important points to remember:

(1) Know your rights, both as author and publisher. The book industry is contract-driven and rights-driven. Know what you can reasonably win in a negotiating situation, or when you have the right to bare your fangs. Subsidiary rights sales, not book sales, are where your biggest income possibilities can come. If you've published one book, you are eligible for membership in the Authors' Guild, a good source of information on changing authors' rights and legal remedies in these changing times. Don't be afraid to ask experts for advice.

(2) Know the nuts and bolts of the publishing process. Writers aiming to self-publish—especially new ones—often come to me with questions. I'm amazed at how many of them, even those with publishable manuscripts, don't have a clue about what publishing involves. They're like a homeowner trying to build a

house without a contractor or blueprints.

One elderly gay gentlemen had the idea that he could take his wonderful hand-typed, much-scribbled-on manuscript to a local printer, and get back a printed book with no further effort on his part. The mother of a well-known gay man who died of AIDS had already done a great job on book design, but paid too high a print bill because she didn't know about bidding jobs. She also didn't know that wholesalers could save her from peddling the book to stores herself. Several would-be authors needed to know that their desktop covers wouldn't make it in today's cutting-edge book design market. Indeed, ama-teurish covers are the hallmark of an amateur in this business and will almost guarantee rejection by major stores and wholesalers.

(3) Know how to find the necessary capital. Small presses and personal imprints that are undercapitalized wind up getting into debt. Then they go bankrupt when cash flow falters and interest payments get out of hand and there's no bailout money. A capital reserve is your bailout. Try to stay out of bank debt. A handful of small presses have found creative alternatives in being nonprofits or co-ops. Wildcat happened because of capital from my mother's estate—a serendipitous happening, because she supported my aim to be a writer since I was ten years old.

(4) Know how to be a businessperson. Some authors (including yours truly, in the past) would like an ivory tower where they can write uninterrupted, save for calls from their agent about the latest windfalls in royalties. But in real life, ivory towers are built on sand, and not every agent represents a client with such devoted passion. In today's intensely competi-tive market, with hundreds of thousands of titles blizzarding the stores every year, a new book may not get major notice without targeted marketing and PR. Without a solid wholesale/distribution strategy, your book won't be in the stores—and, given today's eco-nomic shakiness, you may sell it but not col-lect your receivables unless you get tough. So you have to learn the subsidiary rights/whole-sale/marketing/promotion/production side of things, and how they all interface—or you will go down faster than the Titanic.

My sixteen years as a book editor at the *Reader's Digest,* including all the time I spent on book promotion, design, and manufacturing, gave me valuable experience. But the wholesale side was a mystery to me till 1994.

(5) Know how to put together a good staff, however small. You can't do everything alone. Wildcat has independent contractors for every-thing from office management to cover design. While we stand almost alone in community publishing as a woman/man limited partner-ship, most of our publishing team are women, including sales manager Jacqueline Londe and typesetter Barbara Brown.

For temporary jobs, like mailings, we support local lesbian, gay, bisexual, and transgender youth. Kids learn basic office skills and disci-plines with us, and go off with a letter of rec-ommendation if they do well.

(6) Know when you need lawyers—and when you don't. No contract today should be signed without an attorney's okay. Time and again, I have seen people try to save money on legal fees and write amateur little contracts that don't stand up. On the other hand, you don't need a lawyer for everything. Recently, we brought in $30,000 in long-overdue receiv-ables from stores and wholesalers by hiring an independent contractor who specializes in last-ditch collections. And it's always handy to have an agent for the moments when you need one. For me, that agent remains Mitch Douglas at ICM.

In short:

If you learn about publishing, and learn from your mistakes (without undue financial loss), an author can build a successful enterprise around your work. Inevitably, you may wind up publishing other authors as well. Wildcat does hope to broaden our author scope soon. A major first novel will be Tyler St. Mark's *The Gay Messiah,* planned for publication in 1998.

Meanwhile, we support young authors by jointly maintaining an award-winning Web publication, *The YouthArts Project* (http://www.qcc.org/yap and http://dolphin.upenn.edu/~lgba/youtharts). Our YouthArts co-publishers are Darin Weeks and John Waiblinger. Here, we are proud to showcase the work of Gabriel Baltazar, Ruben "Sick Pig" Gomez, Sean Horton, Juno Parrenas Salazar, Christine Soto, and others.

As Wildcat leaps toward cat-hood, we are concerned about the growing censorship climate in the country. This is why I personally challenged the Justice Department on the CDA/Internet issue and became a plaintiff in the ACLU/ALA case now before the Supreme Court. If the CDA and similar state laws are allowed to stand, there will be a nationwide chill. The Justice Department's latest brief makes it clear that the federal government is looking to take broadened censorship power in all media. This, in combination with religious right efforts to censor books, will surely wreak havoc in gay and lesbian publishing. Wildcat Press is also concerned about industry practices like unlimited returns, slow payments, chargebacks, voodoo accounting, etc. that are hard on independent presses. Recently Wildcat joined the growing numbers of presses who limit returns and give no credit on damaged books. Meanwhile, we think it's important to be activists. We participate in the Publishing Triangle and the Feminist Publishers Network.

We sparked the creation of the Independent Press Coalition, a broad-based new group that seeks innovative methods and venues for getting small-press books into book buyers' hands.

Today, it's a fact that small press books comprise the bulk of titles carried by major jobbers like Ingram. More and more, we authors and we smaller publishers have some power in the industry. The challenge is knowing how to use that power—wisely and effectively.

Patricia Nell Warren has published all kinds of writing. Over forty years, she put out six novels with Dial Press, William Morrow, Bantam, Penguin, and Ballantine. She also published a scholarly work with Harvard/University of Toronto, as well as award-winning short stories, magazine articles, and commentaries. She was a *Reader's Digest* editor for twenty-two years, as well as a *Runner's World* staff writer for women's running. An excerpt from *The Front Runner* is included with works by Homer, Stephen Crane, Jules Verne, and others in Crown's recent major anthology, *Greatest Sports Stories of All Time.*

Schloop, Spooge, Spunk: A Syntax of Sex

by Scott O'Hara

"What's the hardest part of writing porn?" people ask me. Foregoing the obvious double entendre, I prefer the more literal "Learning to type with one hand."

In reality, writing porn doesn't differ noticeably from other forms of writing. You still need to observe all the basic rules (at least, to the extent that you want people to understand you; William S. Burroughs didn't worry about such technicalities, and he seems to have done all right). The problem is that some writers seem to forget the basics, figuring it's "just porn—no one will notice." And, well, they may be right; but it's my contention that porn doesn't have to be "just porn." It can be great writing, too—and why not? Hence, a few reminders.

Give your readers some credit. They've got imaginations. Give them some exercise. It's my contention that anyone who reads a book, even the most basic of books, has to have an imagination. The others are watching videos. So let them romp a little bit. Just because it's porn doesn't mean that you have to tell them everything. Sometimes implication is more titillating than description.

Words are everything. Hey, that's all you've got, when you're writing porn: only words. Use them. Use them all. Your fellow pornographers (and many readers) will undoubtedly snicker at the more exotic usages—you know, "throbbing man-spear," and so forth—but the fact is, seeing the word "dick" repeated sixteen times on one page is even more grating. No matter how much you fetishize jockstraps, there's only a

certain number of times you can read the word before it loses all meaning. And while we're on the subject:I know there are many people out there who object to the nouveau-coinage of "cum," as either a verb or noun, to describe that ultimate product of pornography. I'm not one of them. For chrissakes, folks, we've got few enough words in the English language that are specifically sexual, specifically intended to arouse: prurient words. *Cum* is one of them. "Come" is an attempt to disguise porn as "respectable" writing; I can't read it without adding, mentally, "Lassie." "Cum" is charged with a different meaning, a practically primeval meaning. My appreciation of it is increased by the fact that the distinction is only obvious on the printed page: it is a purely literary invention. Use it. Use jism, too, or jiz, or jizzom, or jazz, or however you want to spell it; use spunk, and spooge, and all the other invented words you can come up with. If it sounds sexy to you, quite likely it will sound sexy to your readers. No one's written the stylebook for pornographers yet, so you're free to invent your own. "Glory hole" or "gloryhole"? You decide.

Which brings us to the bottom line of porn: write what turns you on. I never write a porn story unless I have a hard-on; I can't imagine doing so. If it doesn't even turn you on, how the hell do you expect it to turn other people on? This doesn't mean that you have to write the same story, over and over; I keep coming up (not "cumming" up, thank you) with new fantasies every day. My basic rule is to follow my dick into a story. I don't plot it out in advance; I just keep trying to imagine what twist will turn me on the most. Usually it has something to do with the unexpected, the unusual, and often the irrelevant. Whenever I start getting too close to cumming (yes!), I always try to throw in a digression, something to slow the reader down, to puzzle him a little, maybe even infuriate him. Frustration is the biggest turn-on I can think of.

Finally, and this is the point on which many, if not most, porn writers really fall down: Don't lose your sense of humor. Sex is fun, for crying out loud—or at least it should be. It's also frequently absurd, comical, and incredibly anticlimactic. I'm not saying that you have to make the sex in your stories as farcical as the sex you had last night; just remember that your basic function is as an entertainer. Sex is entertainment; so is humor. They mix remarkably well. There's a writer who has a particular trademark style, which includes the mention of "Lake Lothario" and "Oleander Avenue." I've read entire books of his, waiting for the key words to show up; this man has a sense of humor about his writing, and he doesn't let it stand in the way of describing some real down-and-dirty, quirky, kinky sex. Is it literature? I'll leave that for the literary historians to decide. It sure makes me splooge.

Scott O'Hara is the author of two books: *Do-It-Yourself Piston Polishing (for Non-Mechanics)*, published by Badboy, and *Autopornography*, now available from Haworth/Harrington Park Press. He's also appeared in more than twenty-five videos.

FROM PRINT TO THE INTERNET:
VISIBILITIES, THE ON-LINE LESBIAN MAGAZINE

by Susan Chasin

In 1986, a few friends and I sat around a coffee table discussing the sad lack of a quality lesbian publication for the New York City area. At the time, I assumed it was just another typical coffee-table discussion. But when I left that table, I couldn't let go of the idea. It seemed so important an idea, and it had caught my mind, my heart, and my soul. The problem, of course, was a complete lack of funds to make this idea into a reality.

Shortly afterward, a friend loaned me a copy of a news magazine that contained some article or another that was interesting. Just what that article was I have long since forgotten, but a different article jumped off the pages—an article about the new field of desktop publishing. Suddenly, what was only an idea had the possibility of becoming a reality, one that wouldn't require huge amounts of up-front capital.

This was the beginning of what became *Visibilities*, the lesbian magazine. It began as an idea for a New York City area magazine and soon spread nationally, as people heard about what we were doing.

Frankly, there was always an element of unreality about the whole project. I had hoped that it would succeed; I even had dreams that one day it would pay for itself and perhaps that we could even pay everyone who was working on it. But the reality was much different.

Putting flyers around New York City gained us some writers; I enlisted lots of friends to write, some known, some unknown, but all good. We gained an interview with Marion Zimmer Bradley, the author of *The Mists of Avalon,* based on the mere idea of this magazine. Everyone who heard about the project helped spread the word, and soon we had a small staff of volunteers. For the creative work, that is. It seemed we could never get anyone to help with the scut work: opening mail, processing subscriptions, and most important, selling advertising. This last was the one area that was always to be a paid position, because the women would work on commission. But we never got anyone who was able to sell ads, at least at the beginning. Toward the end we did have a professional salesperson, but *Visibilities* was a hard sell. Major mainstream advertisers, the people with the advertising budgets, didn't want to know about a lesbian publication. Gay men's publications were something else, but there was a perception then that lesbians didn't have money to purchase expensive items. We were not considered a viable market, no matter how much information to the contrary we could provide.

And therein lay the seeds of our eventual downfall.

The only advertisers we could attract were those within the "community." That meant lesbians who owned businesses, bookstores, bed and breakfasts, the occasional lawyer, psychologist, or accountant. These were all businesses that had small advertising budgets, if they actually had any budgets at all. It was inexpensive to advertise in the print version of *Visibilities,* and multiple placements had even better terms. We had our fair share of community advertisers, but ultimately, hard financial times hit everyone.

Try as we might to educate lesbian businesses that in economic hard times you must advertise extensively to increase sales, the message never got through. And to make matters worse, all at once nearly all our advertisers and bookstore outlets stopped paying their bills. No matter how much we begged, pleaded, or demanded, it had no effect. So, with no money coming in, we had no choice but to simply stop publishing. That was in 1991, after five years in print. We'd had our run; we'd done something good, and now it was time simply to leave.

During the time we published there were also lots of good things that happened. We were the first national lesbian publication (perhaps the first publication of any kind) to discuss openly the potential threat of AIDS to lesbians. We were able to meet and talk with very special women: singer Alix Dobkin, who I happened to meet in a Washington, D.C., bookstore, and who agreed to an interview on the spot; Deborah Glick, who ran for the New York State legislature as an open lesbian, and who continues to serve today; Marion Zimmer Bradley, a wonderful writer, who granted us an interview before we even existed, and who graciously came to my dark, Lower East Side apartment to share an unforgettable afternoon over homemade soup; and Audre Lorde, who knows no comparison. We were able to provide our readers with insightful, intelligent, and well-written stories about these women, and more. Frankly, we had fun doing what we did, even with all the problems.

In the years that followed, my life partner would periodically ask me to re-start *Visibilities,* and my answer was always a resounding "no." I wasn't interested in the hassles that running that kind of business entailed. Once was enough. I missed the writing and editing and the contact with the women involved, but now I knew what I hadn't known at the start of *Visibilities*—if you can't pay your staff, the hassles will wear you down.

In the interim we had left the United States. We are living in Israel, and putting together this kind of operation from another continent just wasn't feasible. That is, until my life took another unexpected turn. Part of my "regular" job involved learning how to work with the Internet.

One day in 1996, when we were driving to a town about an hour away from home, my partner again raised the issue of reviving *Visibilities.* When I, yet again, responded with a definite "no," she thought about it and said, "Well, why not do it on the Internet?" Yet again, technology had come to the rescue of an idea—in its time it was desktop publishing; this time it was the Internet.

We talked about it, and all of a sudden the project became viable. I sent e-mail messages to friends who had worked on the print version, and Elynor Vine, who had been an editor, jumped right on the bandwagon. All we needed to get started was free server space because, again, lack of funds was a problem. Once we had decided that we wanted to do this, I sent e-mail messages to friends and told them we needed server space, and if they had any suggestions, we were interested. After a while, a friend in California sent me an e-mail message telling me about a woman in Georgia who was starting a lesbian and gay site, and she put me in touch with her. Becky Boone, the owner of what became Q-World (http://www.qworld.org), saw a copy of the print version of *Visibilities* and was more than happy to donate server space. We were on our way again.

Publishing a magazine on the Internet is an interesting experience, quite different from publishing a print version. For one thing, we went into this as a labor of love, for the fun of it. Money wasn't an issue once Becky became involved; all that was involved was our time and energy and local phone calls here in Israel to put the files on the server in the United States.

Additionally, circulation isn't a worry. At this writing, I have no idea how many women check our site daily, weekly, or monthly. I don't care. So long as Q-World is willing to have us around, we have the energy, the women are willing to write, and people are checking out our pages, we'll keep going.

And the focus of the magazine has changed. In print, although we had some limited international circulation, it was never intended to be an international publication—it was American, and that was that. The Internet version, however, does strive to be international, both in focus and in content. For one thing, since I no longer live in the United States, I have come to understand, even more than I had before, how America-centered American publications are. That's okay, but it's not what I want to see anymore. There are too many points of view, too many interesting lives and stories in the world, and I want to read about them. My hope is that others do as well.

That's easier said than done, though. It has proven very difficult to attract writers from other parts of the world, if those writers are not native English speakers. In on-line discussions with those writers, it has become clear that at least some of them prefer to spend their energy writing their stories, not translat-

ing them. I can certainly understand this. But our lack of funds prevents us from hiring translators, and so our site does not always reflect the international diversity I would prefer.

On the other hand, we can be much more current than we ever were in print. We had such a long turnaround time (we published bimonthly) that we couldn't publish anything that was time sensitive. On the Internet, we can publish information almost instantaneously. News releases are now often distributed via e-mail, and we are on several lesbian and gay organizations' e-mail lists. Once the e-mail arrives, it takes very little time to organize the material for placement on the site.

Our submissions are likewise by e-mail. From a technical point of view, that means a lot less work for us, as there is no typing involved. The coding necessary is fairly simple, and it doesn't take too long to code an average-length article for placement. We have no lack of trouble attracting writers in some areas, poetry most noticeably. In others, however, there seems to be less interest. We started the on-line version with a section for feature articles, which we had in the print version as well, but aside from two articles at the beginning, we were unable to maintain that part of the site. It may be that this is also a function of the Internet itself, that people don't necessarily wish to read longer pieces on-line, and thus writers are not interested in writing them. In any event, at this writing, we have removed that section from the site. Should women desire to contribute feature articles, we can always add the section again.

One of the problems we face now is identical to a problem we had with the print version—a lack of graphic artists. I had hoped that this version would have a lot more artwork than it does, especially as we can now publish in full color, but so far at least, it has been very hard

to attract graphic artists. Even the home page
has had its share of graphic problems. The
original page was designed and drawn by me,
and is therefore not terribly artistic. The only
decent artwork on the page is the logo, which
was designed by a woman at Q-World. At this
writing, we are finally about to change our
home page design, courtesy of Diana Lee, a
graphic artist living in New York.

This is the beauty of this new technology. I
am in a small town in Israel, Elynor is in New
York City, our first fiction contributor lives in
Japan, the designer of our new home page is
in New York, and our contributors live in countries all over the world. We have sections to
which our readers can contribute as well—
travel, recipes, and so forth—and they have. I
may never meet any of these people face-to-
face, yet they are all active contributors to a
vision of quality for the worldwide lesbian
community, thanks to the electronic wonder
that is the Internet.

Visibilities, the on-line lesbian magazine, is
located at:http://www.wowwomen.com/
Visibilities/visib_home.html

GETTING PUBLISHED IN QUEER MAGAZINES

by Shannon Turner, Curve Magazine

Another bland "no thanks" letter.

But why? you wail. What's wrong with it?

Usually, nothing at all is wrong with the work. Most of the pieces that we turn down are well-crafted, thoughtful, and interesting. What's "wrong" is simply that the piece did not fit the very specific editorial guidelines of a queer magazine.

It breaks my heart to send out form-letter rejections, not only because they are so discouraging to writers, but also because they don't give writers the opportunity to revise their work into something that would be really perfect for our publication. Unfortunately, I don't always have the time to compose detailed responses, even when a particular submission really moves me.

In this essay I hope to sketch out an open letter to all the writers I couldn't adequately respond to, exploring some of the most common reasons why pieces are rejected, and identifying some of the key ingredients that publishable pieces share.

Don't Overuse the First Person

Perhaps 80 percent of the pieces we reject are first-person, anecdotal stories about the author's personal experiences. Some of them are truly masterpieces, and would be snapped up readily by a different sort of publication.

But queer magazines, for the most part, are interested in trends. We want to give our readers the scoop on what's happening now, where the community is headed, what spicy little tidbit they will need to know to keep a finger on the pulse of the community. Chances are slim that a first-person story will meet these editorial guidelines, even if the work is so powerful that it reduces our whole staff to laughter or to tears.

So what do you do when something truly exciting or funny happens in your life and you are itching to tell your fellow queers all about it? Try these options on for size:

(1) To begin with, if you find yourself in goofy, tragic, or titillating situations on a regular basis, you should consider becoming a newspaper columnist. First-person anecdotes are bread and butter to opinion editors, and they may well delight in what you have to offer.

(2) Consider submitting to an anthology or a literary journal—you will find dozens of calls for submissions in your local queer newspaper(s), in the national queer press, and in this book.

(3) If you really have your heart set on submitting to a queer magazine, don't despair. You can build on your own experiences to come up with a terrific magazine-style article.

First, think carefully about how your experiences reflect a greater trend that is sweeping the community. Brainstorm a list of events that evidence the trend. Review your list from historical, political, sociological, and/or economic perspectives, to see if you missed anything. Try to come up with a few queer celebrities who are at the forefront of what you've described.

As long as you have several examples that

establish the relevance of what you have to say, anecdotal evidence from your own life will be more than welcome. Indeed, it will spice up your piece and add color to your writing voice.

Cultivate a Unique Voice

Writing voice may be the other key ingredient besides content when it comes to crafting a publishable piece. While newspaper writers consistently strive for an objective tone ("just the facts, ma'am"), magazine writers readily embellish their work with coy vignettes that suggest a raised eyebrow, an approving glance, a horrified stare. A unique, appealing, and colorful writing voice will be your ultimate asset.

Also, remember that every publication has its own attitude and style. When deciding where to send your work, you should consider whether your voice would be compatible with the overall personality of the publication.

Know Your Publications

It really isn't a good idea to submit blind to a magazine you've never seen. Doing so is usually the fastest path to rejection, because it's unlikely that your writing voice, article topic, or cover letter will accurately mirror the style and content of the publication.

Not that you should conform to someone else's style. Rather, you should actively seek out and submit to magazines that publish the kind of work you are interested in writing. Don't waste your time with the rest. As you peruse several different publications that you are considering, ask yourself the following questions about each one:

- Do I like this magazine? Does it speak to me?
- Would I feel proud to appear in it as a contributor?
- What kinds of articles does this magazine generally publish?
- Does each issue of the magazine revolve around a particular theme, or do the editors look for a balance of various themes?
- What's the overall tone like? Is it whimsical? Dark? Academic?
- Does the magazine cover politics? News? Arts and entertainment? Sports?
- What's already been done?
- What seems to be missing?
- Is there a gap that I could fill?

Not only will these questions help you decide which publications resonate with your own personality and writing style, they will also help you get a feel for which publications are likely to take an interest in your work.

A Few Other Pointers

General Rage Doesn't Sell

When submitting to the queer press, avoid writing about your general anger and frustration with respect to homophobia, racism, sexism, and all the other intersections of oppression that impact our lives. It's been done. A lot. While an angry piece can be stirring (and publishable), you should be careful to either focus on a very specific topic or draw a new, surprising conclusion.

Invest in Spell-Check

Simply put, it is highly cost-effective for editors to contract with writers who always turn in polished copy. If you aren't sure about the finer points of grammar and punctuation, have a savvy friend look over your work for you.

While many writers assume that their core ideas are far more important than their mechanics, the reality is that attention to detail can make the difference between acceptance and rejection. Just as a fine work of art looks infinitely more valuable in an attractive frame, the written word seems more energetic and compelling when its syntax and grammar have been polished to a professional sheen.

Give an E-mail Address

An e-mail address can be important when submitting to the national press. Not only is it cheaper and often easier for editors and publishers to communicate with you that way, but also you will probably get a faster response than you would by snail mail.

Send query letters or unsolicited manuscripts by e-mail only if your are specifically asked to do so.

A Final Note

Show me a writer who's gotten a lot of rejection letters and I'll show you a writer with the potential to be wildly successful in this industry. Why? Because he or she has the kind of dogged determination that it takes to survive in the ego-shattering world of publishing.

While popular wisdom might have it that the truly great writers got where they are because of their exquisite raw talent, my experience has been that self-confidence and persistence are equally important.

Don't be afraid to keep sending out your work.

Shannon Turner has done editing and writing in both the mainstream and the queer press for many years. She currently works as the assistant editor at *Curve Magazine*, one of the nation's best-selling lesbian magazines, and at *Dykespeak/ ICON*, San Francisco's popular lesbian newspaper.

GETTING THE WORD OUT: AN AUTHOR'S GUIDE TO PUBLICITY

by Gail Leondar-Wright, Publicist

You've finally completed your book, and even better, you've seen it published. The work of bringing it to the attention of potential readers, however, has just begun. As a newly published author, you will probably want to sell books, communicate your ideas to people who may never read your book, make your name more recognizable among readers and people in the book industry, and demonstrate to your current and possible future publishers that you are willing to promote your work.

As a book publicist, I help authors meet these goals. Sometimes I am employed by publishers who want special attention for a particular title. More often, however, I am hired by authors who are concerned that their publishers will not be able to generate sufficient book reviews and radio, television, and print interviews.

You may assume that publicizing your book is your publisher's responsibility. And to some extent, this is true. However, the degree to which publishers are able and willing to do this varies.

At one extreme, your publisher may be able to do little more than send review copies of your book to book review editors and freelance book reviewers. Lesbian and gay presses usually have solid relationships with queer newspapers and are often able to generate book reviews by doing little else. This is a important part of a good publicity campaign, but it will do nothing to generate radio and television interviews or reviews and interviews in the mainstream press.

On the other hand, if you are being published by a house with plentiful resources, and if your book is one of the lead titles for the season, your publisher may send you out on a book tour—flying you all over the country and arranging for you to be interviewed on television and radio at each of your stops. Don't laugh. It happens.

Most authors find that their publisher's publicity plans fall somewhere in between these two extremes. If you want significant publicity for your book, you must find out what your publisher plans to do to promote your book and, if necessary, find ways to supplement its efforts.

A few months before your book is released, determine who will be responsible for publicizing your book. At a small press, this might be the publisher. At a large house, this will be one of a number of publicists. In my experience, people who publicize books are talented, bright, and hardworking. Your goal is to get information and to share ideas, not to pressure your publicist. Try to establish a respectful working relationship with your publicist. While your publicist may not be the one making decisions about the scope of your publicity campaign, he or she usually has some discretion about how much effort goes into each book. Treat your publicist well, starting with the initial conversation and throughout the publicity campaign.

Find out what your publicist plans to do in order to generate media attention for your book. Will he or she:

- Send review copies to the press?
- Follow up on the mailings to encourage book reviews?
- Try to obtain print, radio, and television interviews in your local area?
- Set up radio interviews via telephone?
- Send you out on a book tour?

Bear in mind that publicists do not know ahead of time which specific media outlets will express interest in your book. You are trying to learn something about the scope of effort, not the scope of results.

If it seems as though your publicist's plans are less than ambitious, you have three options:

1. Try to encourage your publicist to expand the campaign. You are likely to have the most success if you ask for very specific things and offer your assistance. For example you may ask, "Would you be willing to call the three top-rated radio stations in my hometown? I will provide you with contact names and numbers as well as a list of six questions I could answer during the interview."

2. Become your own publicist. There are a number of books that take you through the process. John Kremer's *1001 Ways to Market Your Books* has a good section on publicity. Publicizing your own book can be an enormously empowering experience.

3. Hire a publicist. As when hiring any professional, ask your friends for recommendations of good publicists. There are a lot of us out there, and most are capable and honest. When you find someone who seems to understand and appreciate your book and who seems to know how to publicize books similar to yours, ask for references. Ask for a list of the books your potential publicist has promoted, copies of

print media he or she has obtained, and a list of radio and television producers and hosts with whom the publicist has relationships.

Do not allow yourself to be impressed by the fact that your potential publicist charges large fees. A large fee does not necessarily indicate a better publicist. If money is tight, inform the publicists you are interviewing. I have a sliding scale. So do some others.

Negotiate with your new publicist so that he or she is not replicating the services your publisher will provide for free. For example, if your publisher will try to get book reviews, but will not arrange interviews for you while you are on vacation in California, hire your new publicist to do just that.

Make sure you tell your publisher that you have hired an independent publicist. It is very important that you communicate that this is not because of any dissatisfaction from the in-house publicist's work (if indeed this is true), but rather because you understand that your book is just one of many and that your desires for publicity cannot be completely satisfied in-house. If you handle this conversation with grace, your in-house publicist will most likely welcome a new addition to the team.

Then enjoy having a publicist who assertively advocates on your behalf. A good independent publicist can open doors you never knew existed. He or she can make publicizing your book a joy and can help you establish your name as one people know and remember.

Gail Leondar-Wright is the founder of gail leondar public relations, which helps progressive authors get media attention for their recently published books. She welcomes your questions about book publicity. You can reach her at glpr@aol.com or at (617) 648-1658.

THE WORLD WIDE WEB

by Edisol W. Dotson

Among other things, the World Wide Web is a place where writers can publish their work. There are several on-line publications that accept on-line submissions of fiction, nonfiction, poetry, essay, and other forms of writing, and that are resources for gay and lesbian writers and the community as a whole.

As most writers know only too well, getting published in traditional hard-copy venues can be frustrating and difficult. On the Web, this is not necessarily true. Not because on-line publications are any less particular about the material they accept and publish, but more because a writer can create her or his own web site and therefore publish her or his own material. With persistent and well-thought-out marketing of a web site, a writer's site can be seen by hundreds, if not thousands or millions, of on-line viewers.

Creating a web site is simply a matter of learning a programming language known as HTML (hypertext markup language). HTML is not difficult to learn. There are many software programs available that have simplified website creation (Microsoft Frontpage, HotDog, HTML Pro, WebEdit, to name only a few). Many of these HTML software programs are available as freeware or shareware. The best place to find them on the Web is at http://www.share-ware.com, where you can do a keyword search using "html" to locate and download them.

I created a web site for *Common Fire,* a 'zine I write and publish a few times a year. Go to http://www.sirius.com/~edisol/common.html to get an idea of how to publish on the Web.

Remember that creativity is without limits on the Web.

A few other Web publications of interest to gay and lesbian writers:

Oasis Magazine, an on-line magazine for lesbians, gays, bisexuals, transgenders, and youth.
http://www.oasismag.com

Sapphic Ink, a lesbian literary journal, quarterly Web magazine.
http://www.lesbian.org/sapphic-ink
There is also a hotlist at this site of other websites of interest to lesbian writers.
http://www.lesbian.org/sapphic-ink/hotlist.html

Electronic Gay Community Magazine
http://www.awes.com/egcm/

Q-world's online 'zine, *Qzine*
http://www.qworld.org/QZine/QZine.html

Lesbian-Writer's Webpage
http://www.lesbian.org/lesbian-writers/index.html

Blithe House Quarterly, a web site for short gay fiction.
http://www.spectra.net/~aalvarez/BHQ.html

Another way of finding gay- and lesbian-related writing/publishing web sites is by using the search engines. With search engines you can search by keywords (such as "gay and lesbian writing") and get a list of documents containing those key words. The two best search engines are Excite (http://www.excite.com) and Yahoo (http://www.yahoo.com). Yahoo has a separate section on gay, lesbian, and bisexual resources, and within that section there is a subsection on news and media (http://www.yahoo.com/Society_and_Culture/Lesbians_Gays_and_Bisexuals/News_and_Media/).

Publishing on the Web is an inexpensive alternative to hard-copy publishing. It also gives you complete control of your work, its content and its artistic representation. Few writers have this luxury in more traditional means of publishing.

There are many listings in this book that have web sites. I would encourage you to visit these sites as they give, in some cases, more detailed information on submission guidelines, manuscript prepration, etc. Visiting a web site is also a good way to see what the publications or publishers do or do not publish, something that is very important when submitting work to potential publishers.

Abbreviations and Symbols

The following abbrevations and symbols are used in this book.

* Indicates new listing for this edition.

IRC International Reply Coupon (used for return postage when mailing to Canada or Europe).

MS Manuscript.

MSS Manuscripts.

SAE Self-addressed envelope.

SASE Self-addressed, stamped envelope.

Book Publishers

ACACIA BOOKS
P.O. Box 3630
Berkeley, CA 94703
(510) 451-9559

Publishes lesbian nonfiction, academic, histori-cal, religious, and spirituality subjects. Publishes 1–2 books per year. Letter of query (with SASE) should precede MS submission. Pays royalties. Tips: "Consider establishing a publishing company to self-publish if all doors seem closed. Believe in yourself. Use the library for how-to information on publishing."

ALAMO SQUARE PRESS
P.O. Box 14543
San Francisco, CA 94114
(415) 863-7410
Fax: (415) 863-7456
E-mail: alamosqdist@earthlink.net
Bert Herrman

Publishes lesbian and gay nonfiction, spiritual-ity, and works of social importance to the gay and lesbian community. Offers MS guidelines. Receives 50 MS and query submissions per year. Publishes 2 books per year. Offers book catalog (send for it with business-size enve-lope and 1 first-class stamp). Letter of query should precede MS submission. Responds to MS and query submissions in 2–4 weeks. Accepts MSS not represented by agents. Does not accept unsolicited MSS. Accepts MSS that are simultaneous submissions. Returns MSS with SASE. MSS should be no longer than 250 pages. MSS should be typed or computer gen-erated. Has an average annual overall market-ing budget of $2,000. Has an average per-book marketing budget of $1,000. Payment is nego-tiable. Tips: "Write to a specific market. Ask yourself why anyone should buy your book, beyond the fact that it's wonderful. The gay market is becoming very competitive."

ALYSON PUBLICATIONS, INC.
P.O. Box 4371
Los Angeles, CA 90078
(213) 871-1225
Greg Constante

Publishes lesbian and gay fiction, nonfiction, and erotica. Offers MS guidelines (send for them with business-size envelope and 1 first-class stamp). Receives 1,500 MS and query submissions per year. Prefers letter with syn-opsis and sample chapters be submitted prior to entire MS. Publishes 40 books per year. Offers book catalog (free on request). Letter of query (with SASE) should precede MS submis-sion. Responds to MS and query submissions in 3 months. Accepts MSS not represented by agents. Accepts unsolicited MSS. Does not accept MSS that are simultaneous submissions. Returns MSS with SASE. MSS should be typed, double-spaced. Letter-quality preferred. Pays royalties but prefers to negotiate with individ-ual writers. Alyson Publications has one imprint, Alyson Wonderland, a line of books for the children of gay and lesbian parents.

AUNT LUTE BOOKS
P.O. Box 410687
San Francisco, CA 94141
(415) 558-8116
Joan Pinkvoss

Publishes multicultural fiction and nonfiction.
Offers MS guidelines (free on request).
Receives 200–300 MS and query submissions
per year. Publishes 3–4 books per year. Offers
book catalog (free on request). Letter of query
(with SASE) should precede MS submission.
Responds to queries in 2–3 weeks. Responds
to MS submissions in at least 3 months.
Prefers MSS not represented by agents. Accepts
unsolicited MSS. Prefers MSS that are not
simultaneous submissions. Returns MSS with
SASE. MSS should be typed, double-spaced.
Letter-quality submissions preferred. Pays royalties. Tips: "Don't send out work until it's the
best writing you are capable of. We tend to
work with our authors more than most publishers, but we expect a high level of writing
by the time the work reaches us. We seek manuscripts by women from a variety of cultures,
ethnic backgrounds, and subcultures; women
who are self-aware and who, in the face of all
contradictory evidence, are still hopeful that
the world can reserve a place of respect for
each woman in it."

AUTONOMEDIA/SEMIOTEXTE*
P.O. Box 568
Brooklyn, NY 11211-0568
(718) 963-2603
E-mail: autonobook@aol.com
World Wide Web: http://www.autonomedia.org
Jim Fleming

Publishes lesbian and gay nonfiction, academic,
and spirituality subjects. Publishes 20 books
per year. Receives 150 MS and query submissions per year. Letter of query (with SASE)
should precede MS submission. Responds to
queries in 2 months. Responds to MS submissions in 3 months. Accepts MSS not represented by agents. Accepts unsolicited MSS. Accepts
MSS that are simultaneous submissions. MSS
should by typed, double-spaced.

BAY PRESS
115 West Denny Way
Seattle, WA 98119
(206) 284-5913
Fax: (206) 284-1218
Email: BayPress@aol.com
Kimberly A. Barnett or Sally Brunsman

Publishes lesbian and gay cultural criticism
and critical theory. Publishes 4 books per year.
Offers book catalog (free on request).
Responds to MS and query submissions in 6–8
weeks. Accepts MSS not represented by agents.
Accepts unsolicited MSS. Does not accept MSS
that are simultaneous submissions. Returns
MSS with SASE.

BEACON PRESS
25 Beacon Street
Boston, MA 02108-2800
(617) 742-2110
Fax: (617) 723-3097
Deborah Chasman

Publishes lesbian and gay nonfiction, political,
anthropology, and gender studies. Also publishes historical, religious, and spirituality subjects if book is an academic treatment of these
subjects. Publishes serious nonfiction only.
Author must have academic or other relevant
qualifications. Receives 6,000 MS and query
submissions per year. Publishes 60 books per
year. Offers book catalog (free on request).
Letter of query (with SASE) should precede MS
submission. Responds to MS and query submissions in 12–16 weeks. Does not accept unsolicited MSS. Returns MSS with SASE. MSS
should be $8^{1}/_{2}$ x 11, singled-sided, typed,

double-spaced, letter-quality. No original art-work accepted. Send sample chapter(s). Tips: "Always include a SASE. Write straightforward query letters and describe intended market and comparable books in print. We are not consid-ering fiction, poetry, memoirs, 'inspirational' books, self-help, or 'how-to' books. We are a combination trade/academic publisher; many books we publish have potential in the college course market and will undergo review by scholars in appropriate fields."

BLACK SPARROW PRESS
24 Tenth Street
Santa Rosa, CA 95401
(707) 579-4011
John Martin

Publishes gay, lesbian, nongay, and nonlesbian fiction and poetry. Receives 1,000–1,200 MS and query submissions per year. Publishes 12 books per year. Offers book catalog (free on request). Letter of query (with SASE) should precede MS submission. Responds to queries in 5 days. Responds to MS submissions in 30–60 days. MSS should be sent to Michele Filshie. Accepts MSS not represented by agents. Accepts unsolicited MSS. Does not accept MSS that are simultaneous submissions. Returns MSS with SASE. Pays royalties; offers advances.

BLUESTOCKING BOOKS*
P.O. Box 50998
Irvine, CA 92619-0998
(714) 835-5595
E-mail: m.gillon@juno.com

Publishes lesbian fiction, nonfiction, and acad-emic subjects. Publishes 4–6 books per year. Receives 50 MS and query submissions per year. Responds to MS and query submissions in 3 months. Accepts MSS not represented by agents. Accepts unsolicited MSS. Accepts MSS that are simultaneous submissions. Does not

return MSS. MSS should be typed, double-spaced, one side of paper, 1-inch margins. Pays royalties. Tips: "Manuscripts should be as clean and as finished as possible, no rough drafts or works in progress."

BUA LUANG BOOKS*
P.O. Box 147
Oakland, CA 94604-0147
(510) 465-0747
Fax: (510) 836-0798
E-mail: e_allyn@sirius.com
E. G. Allyn
Samorn Chaiyana

Publishes a wide range of topics on Asia for the general and academic markets (cross-cul-tural research on sexuality, historical, lan-guage/dictionaries, travel, sociology/anthro-pology, etc.). Receives 15 query and MS sub-missions per year. Responds to query submis-sions within 3 weeks. Accepts MSS not repre-sented by agents. Accepts unsolicited MSS (prefers two sample chapters first). Prefers submissions on disk (DOS) in major word pro-cessing programs or as TXT file. Accepts simul-taneous submissions. Returns MSS with SASE. Pays royalties. Tips: "Asian gay and lesbian writers are particularly encouraged to submit. Writers in English as a second language should not be shy about submitting. We're looking for content and fresh voices. We are sensitive to the need of some writers for absolute anonymity. Academic or special-interest works on Asian subjects should also be geared for an international market. Our titles are distributed worldwide."

31

CAILLECH PRESS

482 Michigan Street
St. Paul, MN 55102
(612) 225-9647
E-mail: zahniser@minn.net

Publishes feminist multicultural popular reference and gift books (e.g., books of quotations). Publishes titles for the general reader; no fiction or poetry. Publishes 1 book per year. Offers catalog (free on request). Not currently accepting MSS.

CALYX BOOKS

P.O. Box B
Corvallis, OR 97339
(541) 753-9384
Fax: (541) 753-0515
E-mail: calyx@proaxis.com
Margarita Donnelly

Publishes women's fiction, nonfiction, and poetry. Offers MS guidelines (send for them with business-size envelope and 1 first-class stamp). Receives 400 MS and query submissions per year. Publishes 3–4 books per year. Offers book catalog (free on request). Letter of query (with SASE) should precede MS submission. Responds to queries in 1 month. Responds to MS submissions in 1 year. Accepts MSS not represented by agents. Accepts unsolicited MSS. Accepts MSS that are simultaneous submissions. Do not submit book MS without following guidelines for MS preparation. Offers advances; pays royalties. Tips: "Be familiar with what we've published. Follow our guidelines for manuscript submissions. Please contact publisher about future submission periods."

CAROLINA WREN PRESS

120 Morris Street
Durham, NC 27701
(919) 560-2738

Publishes lesbian fiction, nonfiction, poetry, and children's books. Offers MS guidelines (send for them with 9 x 12 envelope and 50¢ postage). Receives 2,000 MS and query submissions per year. Publishes 3 books per year. Offers book catalog (send for it with 5 x 7 envelope and 2 first-class stamps). Responds to MS and query submissions in 2–3 months. Send fiction MSS to Kathryn Lovatt. Send nonfiction MSS to Charlotte Hoffman. Send poetry MSS to Marilyn Bulman. Send children's book MSS to Ruth Smullin. Accepts MSS not represented by agents. Accepts unsolicited MSS. Accepts MSS that are simultaneous submissions. MSS should be typed, double-spaced. Has an average annual overall marketing budget of $5,000. Has an average per book marketing budget of $1,000. Pays with copies of book. Tips: "Know your publisher and what they are looking for. Send for guidelines and read them. Make sure you know the mechanics of good grammar, sentence structure, and storyline. They are the same regardless of your politics."

CARROLL & GRAF PUBLISHERS, INC.

260 Fifth Avenue
New York, NY 10001
(212) 889-8772
Kent Carroll

Publishes fiction and nonfiction. Receives 5,000 MS and query submissions per year. Publishes 120 books per year. Offers book catalog (send for it with business-size envelope and 1 first-class stamp). Does not accept unsolicited MSS. Only accepts MSS submitted by agents.

CASSELL ACADEMIC*

P.O. Box 605
Herndon, VA 20172-0605
(703) 661-1586
(703) 661-1501
T. J. Johnson

Publishes lesbian and gay nonfiction, academic, poetry, religious, historical, spirituality, and news. Publishes 50–100 books per year. Letter of query should precede MS submission. Accepts MSS not represented by agents. Accepts unsolicited MSS. MSS should be typed, double-spaced. Tips: "Send outline and sample chapters with letter of inquiry. Do not send full manuscript."

CENTURION PRESS*

8306 Wilshire Boulevard, Unit 631
Beverly Hills, CA 90211-2382
(818) 796-0004
Fax: (818) 792-7444
E-mail: centupress@aol.com
Hector Cordova

Publishes gay male travel and entertainment. Letter of query should precede MS submission. Responds to queries in 1 week. Responds to MS submissions in 3–4 weeks. Accepts MSS not represented by agents. Does not accept unsolicited MSS. Does not accept MSS that are simultaneous submissions. Returns MSS. Pays royalties.

CHELSEA HOUSE PUBLISHERS*

Dept. C97, P.O. Box 914
1974 Sproul Road, Suite 400
Broomall, PA 19008-0914
(610) 353-5166
Fax: (610) 353-5191
E-mail: info@chelseahouse.com
Henna Remstein

Publishes lesbian and gay nonfiction. Offers MS guidelines.

CHICORY BLUE PRESS

795 East Street North
Goshen, CT 06756
(860) 491-2271
Fax: (860) 491-8619
Sondra Zeidenstein

Publishes lesbian fiction, nonfiction, and poetry in chapbook length (30–35 pages). Receives 60–90 MS submissions per year. Publishes 1–4 chapbooks per year. Offers book catalog (free on request). Letter of query (with writing sample, 5–10 pages, and SASE) should precede MS submission. Responds to MS and query submissions in 3 months. Accepts MSS not represented by agents. Accepts unsolicited MSS. Accepts MSS that are simultaneous submissions. Returns MSS with SASE. Has an average per-book marketing budget of $200–$500. Pays with 10 copies of book.

CIRCLET PRESS, INC.

1770 Massachusetts Avenue #278
Cambridge, MA 02140
(617) 864-0492
E-mail: circlet-info@circlet.com
Cecilia Tan

Publishes lesbian and gay erotic science fiction short story anthologies. Does not publish novels. Does not accept novel queries. Offers MS guidelines (send for them with business-size envelope and 1 first-class stamp). Accepts MSS from April 15 to August 31 each year. Responds to MS submissions in 4–6 months. Accepts MSS not represented by agents. Accepts unsolicited MSS. Accepts MSS that are simultaneous submissions. Returns MSS with SASE. MSS should be under 15,000 words. Dot-matrix submissions accepted. Has an annual marketing budget of $50,000. Has an average per-book marketing budget of $5,000. Pays .05¢ per word on acceptance. Tips: "No death, no horror, no nonconsensual sex, no clichés.

We are interested in short stories that combine science fiction and erotica. We are not interested in stories that are not erotic or not science fiction. We are interested in alternative sexualities including S/M, leather fetishes, transgender, etc. Please read our MS guidelines prior to submitting MSS."

CITY LIGHTS BOOKS
261 Columbus Avenue
San Francisco, CA 94133
(415) 362-1901
Fax: (415) 362-4921
Robert Sharrard

Publishes lesbian and gay fiction and poetry. Receives 1,000 MS and query submissions per year. Publishes 10–12 books per year. Offers book catalog (free on request). Letter of query should precede MS submissions. Responds to queries in 4 weeks. Responds to MS submissions in 8 weeks. Accepts MSS not represented by agents. Accepts unsolicited MSS. Accepts MSS that are simultaneous submissions. Returns MSS with SASE. Offers advance against royalties.

CLEIS PRESS
P.O. Box 14684
San Francisco, CA 94114
(415) 575-4700
Fax: (415) 575-4705
E-mail: fdcleis@aol.com
Frédérique Delacoste

1997 recipient of the Firecracker Alternative Book Award (Oustanding Press of the Year). Publishes provocative nonfiction and fiction books by women (and a few men). Publishes lesbian and gay studies, sexual politics, self-help, feminism, fiction, erotica, humor, translations of women's literature, human rights, biographies, historical and political subjects, journalism, popular nonfiction. Distributed to

the trade by Publishers Group West. Receives 800 MS and query submissions per year. Publishes 14 books per year. Offers book catalog (send for it with business-size envelope and 2 first-class stamps). Responds to queries in 4–6 weeks. Responds to MS submissions in 4 weeks. Accepts MSS not represented by agents. Returns MSS with SASE. MSS should be $8^1/_2$ x 11, typed, double-spaced. Send list of publications and resume along with book proposal. Pays royalties. Tips: "Give editor two-month 'option' (exclusive), after which writer may submit work to other editors. Do not send poetry or recommendation letters."

COLUMBIA UNIVERSITY PRESS
562 West 113th Street
New York, NY 10025
(212) 666-1000, x7121
Fax: (212) 316-3100
E-mail: am310@columbia.edu
Ann Miller

Publishes lesbian and gay nonfiction targeted primarily toward an academic and gay and lesbian readership. Publishes 3–4 lesbian/gay studies titles per year. Responds to queries in 1 month. Responds to MS submissions in 3 months. Considers MSS not represented by agents. Accepts unsolicited MSS. Accepts MSS that are simultaneous submissions. Returns MSS with SASE. MSS should be typed, double-spaced. Pays royalties.

COMMON COURAGE PRESS
Box 702
Corner 139 & Jackson Road
Monroe, ME 04951
(207) 525-0900

Publishes lesbian and gay nonfiction. Offers MS guidelines (send for them with business-size envelope and 1 first-class stamp). Publishes 12 books per year. Receives more than 200 MS and query submissions per year. Responds to queries in 1 week. Responds to MS submissions in 1 month. Accepts MSS not represented by agents. Accepts unsolicited MSS. Accepts MSS that are simultaneous submissions. Returns MS with SASE.

COMPANION PRESS*

P.O. Box 2575
Laguna Hills, CA 92654
(714) 362-9726
Fax: (714) 362-9726
E-mail: sstewart@companionpress.com

Publishes lesbian and gay nonfiction and erotica. Offers MS guidelines (send for them with SASE). Publishes 6–12 books per year. Has an annual overall marketing budget of $60,000–$120,000. Has an average per-book marketing budget of $10,000. Receives 50–100 MS and query submissions per year. Letter of query (with SASE) should precede MS submission. Responds to MS and query submissions in 30–60 days. Accepts MSS not represented by agents. Does not accept unsolicited MSS. Does not accept MSS that are simultaneous submissions. Returns MSS with SASE. Submit one laser copy and computer disk in text-only format (IBM or Macintosh). Pays royalties. Tips: "We only publish books dealing with sexuality in movies and video, biography, histories, fan books, video guides, etc. Topics include adult, bisexuality, drag, gay, lesbian, nudity, taboos, etc."

CORNELL UNIVERSITY PRESS

Sage House, 512 East State Street
P.O. Box 250
Ithaca, NY 14851
(607) 277-2338
Bernhard Kendler

Publishes lesbian and gay academic and historical subjects; critical and theoretical writing. Offers MS guidelines (free on request).

Receives 1,500–2,000 MS and query submissions per year. Publishes 150 books per year. Offers book catalog (free on request). Query letter should precede MS submission. Responds to queries in 1 week to 10 days. Responds to MS submissions in 12–14 weeks. Considers MSS not represented by agents. Considers MSS that are simultaneous submissions. Returns MSS with SASE. MSS should be typed, double-spaced, one side of page only. Letter-quality submissions preferred. Usually pays royalties; sometimes offers advances. Tips: "We are an academic publisher and publish 'trade' books on occasion; no fiction, no poetry."

DAEDALUS PUBLISHING COMPANY*

584 Castro Street #518
San Francisco, CA 94114
(415) 626-1867
Fax: (415) 487-1137
E-mail: daedalus@bannon.com
World Wide Web:
http://www.bannon.com/daedalus
Race Bannon

Publishes fiction, nonfiction, and erotica. Offers MS guidelines (free on request). Publishes 2–4 books per year. Has an overall annual marketing budget of $15,000. Receives 50 MS and query submissions per year. Letter of query (with SASE) should precede MS submission. Responds to queries in 4–8 weeks. Responds to MS submissions in 2–3 months. Accepts MSS not represented by agents. Accepts unsolicited MSS. Accepts MSS that are simultaneous submissions. Returns MSS with SASE. Pays royalties. Tips: "Always send a letter first. Manuscripts sent without a letter sent beforehand will be returned unread."

DAW BOOKS, INC.
375 Hudson Street, 3rd Floor
New York, NY 10014-3658
Peter Stampfel

Publishes science fiction and fantasy books only. Has published gay and lesbian books within these two genres. Offers MS guidelines (free on request). Publishes 60 books per year. Offers book catalog. Letter of query (with SASE) should precede MS submission. Accepts MSS not represented by agents. Accepts unsolicited MSS. Does not accept MSS that are simultaneous submissions. Returns MSS with SASE. MSS should be 80,000+ words in length. Tips: "Read DAW books to learn what we publish."

DIMI PRESS*
3820 Oak Hollow Lane, S.E.
Salem, OR 97302-4774
(503) 364-7698
Fax: (503) 364-9727
E-mail: dickbook@aol.com
Dick Lutz

Publishes fiction. Offfers MS guidelines (send for them with SASE). Publishes 4–5 books per year. Receives 100 MS and query submissions per year. Letter of query (with SASE) should precede MS submission. Responds to queries in 2 months. Responds to MS submissions in 4 months. Accepts MSS not represented by agents. Accepts unsolicited MSS. Accepts MSS that are simultaneous submissions. Returns MSS with SASE. MSS should be typed, double-spaced. Pays royalties.

DOWN THERE PRESS/YES PRESS
938 Howard Street #101
San Francisco, CA 94103
(415) 974-8985, x105
Fax: (415) 974-8989
E-mail: goodvibe@well.com
Joani Blank

Publishes female erotica (currently only erotic short stories for anthologies in the "Herotica" series) and male and female sexual self-awareness subjects (not exclusively gay). Receives 24 MS and query submissions per year. Publishes 1–2 books per year. Offers book catalog (free on request). Letter of query (with SASE) should precede MS submission. Responds to MS and query submissions in 2 months. Accepts MSS not represented by agents. Accepts unsolicited MSS. Accepts MSS that are simultaneous submissions. MSS should be 8 $^1/_2$ x 11, typed, double-spaced. Dot-matrix submissions accepted. Pays royalties. Tips: "Ideal submission is a one-page cover letter, a descriptive table of contents, summaries of each chapter, and a chapter or two to show how author writes."

DUTTON
A Division of Penguin U.S.A.
375 Hudson Street
New York, NY 10014

Publishes lesbian and gay fiction, popular non-fiction, political, and historical subjects. Publishes over 400 books per year (combined in hardcover/trade and paper/mass market formats). Prefers MSS represented by agents, but will consider unagented MSS. Accepts MSS that are simultaneous submissions. Returns MSS with SASE. MSS should be 8 $^1/_2$ x 11, typed, double-spaced, one side of paper only. No photographic or computer disk submissions accepted. Tips: "Do your research and send your manuscript to the attention of an appropriate editor. Include all your credentials in cover letter, including media/publicity experience you've had."

EIGHTH MOUNTAIN PRESS

624 S.E. 29th Avenue
Portland, OR 97214
(503) 233-3936
Fax: (503) 233-0774
E-mail: soapston@teleport.com
Ruth Gundle

Publishes fiction, essays, nonfiction, and poetry by women. Has a biennial contest for book-length poetry MSS. Offers a $1,000 advance against royalties and publication in the prize series. Send SASE for guidelines to the attention of the Eighth Mountain Poetry Prize. Offers MS guidelines (send for them with business-size envelope and 1 first-class stamp). Receives 500–1000 MS and query submissions per year. Publishes 2 books per year. Offers book catalog (send for it with business-size envelope and 42¢ postage). Letter of query (with SASE) should precede MS submission. Responds to queries in 4–8 weeks. Responds to MS submissions in 2–4 months. Accepts MSS not represented by agents. Accepts unsolicited MSS. Does not accept MSS that are simultaneous submissions. Has an average annual overall marketing budget of $5,000–$6,000. Has an average per-book marketing budget of $2,000–$3,000. Pays royalties. Tips: "Research the publishers and send your queries to the ones that are publishing work like yours. Always send a concise summary and description. The Eighth Mountain Press publishes high-quality feminist literature written by women, in beautifully designed and produced editions."

FANTAGRAPHICS BOOKS, INC./EROS COMIX

7563 Lake City Way
Seattle, WA 98115
(206) 524-1967
Ezra Mark

Publishes some lesbian and gay comics and cartoons. Does not publish prose or poetry. Offers submission guidelines (send for them with business-size envelope and 1 first-class stamp). Receives 250–300 cartoon or comics MS and query submissions per year. Publishes 15–20 books per year. Offers book catalog (free on request). Letter of query (with SASE) should precede MS submission. Responds to MS and query submissions in 1–3 months. Accepts unsolicited MSS. Accepts MSS that are simultaneous submissions. Do not submit original art; originals will be requested upon acceptance. Pays royalties. Tips: "Do not send prose or poetry manuscripts; this just wastes our time. Don't send portfolios or art samples without a story to go with them. We like to see relatively complete work, not works-in-progress. Neatness counts. We like personal, iconoclastic works. Don't send us superhero/action-adventure / sci-fi material. We would much rather see down-to-earth, real material."

FIREBRAND BOOKS

141 The Commons
Ithaca, NY 14850
(607) 272-0000
Nancy K. Bereano

Publishes lesbian and feminist fiction, nonfiction, poetry, erotica, news, and political subjects. Receives 500 MS and query submissions per year. Publishes 8–10 books per year. Offers book catalog (free on request). Responds to queries in 2 weeks. Responds to MS submissions in 2 weeks to 2 months. Accepts MSS not represented by agents. Accepts unsolicited

MSS. Accepts MSS that are simultaneous submissions (with notification only). No handwrit-
ten submissions accepted, except from institu-
tionalized women. Pays royalties. Recipient of
the 1996 Lambda Literary Publisher Service
Award.

FIRST BOOKS, INC.*
2040 N. Milwaukee Avenue
Chicago, IL 60647
(773) 276-5911
World Wide Web: http://www.firstbooks.com

Publishes lesbian and gay nonfiction. Publishes
5 books per year. Responds to MS and query
submissions in 2 weeks. Accepts MSS not represented by agents. Accepts unsolicited MSS.
Accepts MSS that are simultaneous submissions. Returns MSS with SASE.

FLOATING LOTUS BOOKS*
P.O. Box 147
Oakland, CA 94604-0147
(510) 465-0747
Fax: (510) 836-0798
E-mail: e_allyn@sirius.com
E. G. Allyn
Samorn Chaiyana

Publishes primarily Asian/cross-cultural gay-
oriented books. Receives 15 query and MS submissions per year. Responds to query submissions within 3 weeks. Accepts MSS not represented by agents. Accepts unsolicited MSS
(prefers two sample chapters first). Prefers
submissions on disk (DOS) in major word pro-
cessing programs or as TXT file. Accepts simultaneous submissions. Returns MSS with SASE.
Pays royalties. Tips: "Asian gay and lesbian
writers are particularly encouraged to submit.
Writers in English as a second language should
not be shy about submitting. We're looking for
content and fresh voices. We are sensitive to
the need of some writers for absolute anonymity.

Academic or special-interest works on Asian
subjects should also be geared for an international market. Our titles are distributed worldwide."

FOUR WALLS EIGHT WINDOWS
39 W. 14th Street #503
New York, NY 10011
(212) 206-8965
Fax: (212) 206-8799
E-mail: EightWind@aol.com
World Wide Web: http://users.aol.com/spec-
press/fourwalls.htm
John Oakes

Publishes lesbian and gay fiction, nonfiction,
political, and health subjects. Receives 3,000
MS and query submissions per year. Publishes
20 books per year. Offers book catalog (free on
request). Letter of query (with SASE) should
precede MS submission. Responds to queries in
3 weeks. Responds to MS submissions in 3
months. Accepts MSS not represented by
agents. Accepts MSS that are simultaneous
submissions. Returns MSS with SASE. Pays
advances. Tips: "Be patient. Familiarize yourself with what we publish before you submit
something."

GAY SUNSHINE PRESS/LEYLAND PUBLICATIONS
P.O. Box 410690
San Francisco, CA 94141
(415) 626-1935
Winston Leyland

Publishes gay male fiction, nonfiction, erotica,
and historical subjects. Publishes 8–10 books
per year. Offers book catalog (available for
$1). Letter of query (with SASE) should pre-
cede MS submission. Responds to query and
MS submissions in 4–8 weeks. Accepts MSS not

represented by agents. Does not accept unsolicited MSS. Does not accept MSS that are simultaneous submissions. MSS should be typed, double-spaced. Does not accept dot-matrix submissions. Pays royalties or outright purchase.

GLB PUBLISHERS
P.O. Box 78212
San Francisco, CA 94107
(415) 621-8307
W. L. Warner

Publishes gay, lesbian, and bisexual fiction, nonfiction, poetry, and erotica. Receives 10 MS and query submissions per year. Publishes 6 books per year. Book catalog available (free on request). Letter of query should precede MS submission. Responds to queries in 1–2 weeks. Responds to MS submissions in 3–6 weeks. Accepts MSS not represented by agents. Accepts unsolicited MSS. Does not accept MSS that are simultaneous submissions. MS should be typed, double-spaced, letter-quality. Prefers computer disk submissions (IBM). Author pays for printing cost and cover development; publisher pays for and performs the remainder of services. Pays 15%–25% royalty to author when book is sold. Tips: "Since the author contributes to the cost of producing the book, he/she can have considerable input into the appearance of the book and cover. Author should give some thought to the expected size and type of audience. Since we do not pay advances, we are not as demanding of the highest quality, and may accept manuscripts turned down by larger houses."

GUILFORD PUBLICATIONS
72 Spring Street
New York, NY 10012
(212) 431-9800
Peter Wissoker

Publishes lesbian and gay books and journals

on professional and academic subjects only (e.g., mental health, social criticism). Publishes 70 books per year. Offers book catalog (free on request). Letter of query should precede MS submission. Responds to queries in 3–4 weeks. Accepts MSS not represented by agents. Accepts unsolicited MSS. Accepts MSS that are simultaneous submissions. Returns MSS with SASE. MSS should be prepared using the American Psychological Association style. Pays royalties.

HALL CLOSET BOOK COMPANY*
P.O. Box 19335
Seattle, WA 98109
(800) 895-8915
Fax: (206) 286-0656
E-mail: closetbk@aol.com

An audio book publisher publishing gay and lesbian fiction, nonfiction, erotica, religious, and historical subjects. Letter of query (with SASE) should precede MS submission. Accepts MSS not represented by agents. Does not accept unsolicited MSS.

HAWORTH PRESS/HARRINGTON PARK PRESS
10 Alice Street
Binghamton, NY 13904
(607) 722-5857
Fax: (800) HAWORTH
E-mail: getinfo@haworth.com
Sandra Jones Sickels

Publishes lesbian, gay, and biseuxal nonfiction and academic subjects. Offers MS guidelines (free on request). Publishes 215 books per year (approximately 20 books per year on gay/lesbian/bisexual topics). Query letter with 2–3 sample chapters prefered. Responds to queries in 1 month. Responds to MS submissions in 6 weeks. Accepts MSS not represented

39

by agents. Accepts unsolicited MSS. Does not accept MSS that are simultaneous submissions. MSS should be under 300 pages. MSS should be typed, double-spaced. Pays royalties. Also publishes *Journal of Homosexuality, Journal of Lesbian Studies, Journal of Gay and Lesbian Social Services,* and *Journal of Gay and Lesbian Psychotherapy.* See individual listings in "Magazines and Journals" section. Tips: "Our orientation is generally toward scholarly, research-based materials, but we are open to consideration of any nonfiction work."

THE HAWORTH SERIES ON WOMEN
University of Vermont
Department of Psychology/John Dewey Hall
Burlington, VT 05405
(802) 656-4156
Fax: (802) 656-8783
E-mail: e_rothbl@dewey.uvm.edu
Esther D. Rothblum, Ph.D.

Publishes subject matter that pertains to all women, including lesbian women. Publishes nonfiction and academic subjects. Receives 30 MS and query submissions per year. Publishes 5 books per year. Offers book catalog (free on request from Haworth Press, Inc., 10 Alice St., Binghamton, NY 13904-1580). Responds to queries in 2 weeks. Responds to MS submissions in 3 months. Accepts MSS not represented by agents. Accepts unsolicited MSS. Does not accept MSS that are simultaneous submissions. Returns MSS with SASE. MSS should be typed, double-spaced. Dot-matrix submissions accepted. Once MSS is accepted, computer disk is required. Accepts photography submissions. American Psychological Association guidelines must be followed. Negotiates advance upon acceptance, then pays royalties. Tips: "This book series is aimed at an intelligent, well-educated general audience. We look for books

that fall somewhere between 'pop psychology' and highbrow scholarship, and that address women's mental health issues from a feminist perspective."

HAY HOUSE, INC.
P.O. Box 5100
Carlsbad, CA 92019-5100
(619) 431-7695
Fax: (610) 431-6948
E-mail: hayhousesd@hayhouse.com
World Wide Web: http://www.hayhouse.com
Jill Kramer

Publishes self-help subjects. Receives 1,200 MS and query submissions per year. Publishes 20–30 books per year. Letter of query should precede MS submission. Responds to queries in 2–3 weeks. Responds to MS submissions in 1 month. Accepts MSS not represented by agents. Accepts unsolicited MSS. Accepts MSS that are simultaneous submissions. Returns MSS with SASE. MSS should be typed, double-spaced. Pays standard royalties. Tips: "We publish self-help and New Thought books in the areas of psychology, women's issues, the environment, health, relationships, prayer and meditation, business, nutrition, and more. Basically, we look for words with a positive slant that help to heal the planet. No poetry or children's books."

HEALTH ACTION PRESS*
6437 Taggart Road
Delaware, OH 43015
(614) 548-5340
Fax: (614) 548-0388

Publishes health, politics, environmental issues. Does not accept queries or MS submissions. Solicits MSS.

HENRY HOLT & COMPANY, INC.
115 W. 18th Street
New York, NY 10011
(212) 886-9200
Fax: (212) 633-0748

Not an exclusive publisher of lesbian and gay books. Publishes lesbian and gay fiction, nonfiction, and historical subjects. Offers MS guidelines (send for them with any size envelope and 1 first-class stamp). Send proposal plus 2–3 sample chapters. Accepts MSS not represented by agents. Accepts unsolicited MSS. Accepts MSS that are simultaneous submissions. Returns MSS with SASE. MSS should be typed, double-spaced. Payment varies.

HERBOOKS
P.O. Box 7467
Santa Cruz, CA 95061
(408) 425-7493
E-mail: ireti@igc.apc.org
World Wide Web: http://www.igc.apc.org/herbooks/

Publishes feminist fiction and nonfiction with an emphasis on lesbians. We are particularly interested in work by lesbians and women of color. No entry fee. Winner receives publication and $500 and 50 free copies. Publishes 1 book per year. Offers book catalog (send for it with business-size envelope and 1 first-class stamp). Responds to queries in 2 weeks. Responds to MS submissions in 1 month. MSS should be typed, double-spaced. Has an average annual overall marketing budget of $1,000. Has an average per-book marketing budget of $200. Pays 10% royalty every 6 months, plus 40% discount on books, and a negotiated number of free copies. Tips: "Send for publisher's catalog and figure out whether your book fits into our list. For example, HerBooks does not publish work with sadomasochistic content; we do many Jewish lesbian books, etc."

HOT FLASH PRESS
Box 21506
San Jose, CA 95151
(408) 292-1172
Meg Bowman or Jane Turner

Publishes women's and feminist nonfiction, poetry, historical, spirituality, and dramatic readings. Receives 12 query submissions per year. Publishes 1–2 books per year. Letter of query should precede MS submission. Responds to queries in 2 weeks. Responds to MS submissions in 2 months. Accepts unsolicited MSS. Accepts MSS that are simultaneous submissions. Returns MSS with SASE. Offers no payment. Tips: "Interested in feminist materials that can be used for public programs, college classroom readings, church programs that raise consciousness regarding feminism, spirituality, peace, ecofeminism, etc."

INSIGHT BOOKS
233 Spring Street, 5th Floor
New York, NY 10013
(212) 620-8005
Fax: (212) 463-0742
E-mail: frankd@plenum.com
Frank K. Darmstadt

Publishes lesbian and gay academic, historical, and trade nonfiction. Publishes 12 books per year. Receives 5,000 MS and query submissions per year. Letter of query (with SASE) should precede MS submission. Responds to queries in 2 weeks. Responds to MS submissions in 6–8 weeks. Accepts MSS not represented by agents. Accepts unsolicited MSS. Accepts MSS that are simultaneous submissions. Returns MSS with SASE. MSS should be 350 pages, typed, double-spaced. Advances offered between $2,500–$7,500; royalties offered annually. Tips: "We are looking for writers who are passionate about their work, and who are unafraid to allow that passion to infuse their work. The

41

editorial relationship is one of compromise and collaboration, not confrontation."

INSTITUTE OF LESBIAN STUDIES

P.O. Box 25568
Chicago, IL 60625
Fax: (773) 327-4981
Ann Seawall

Publishes lesbian nonfiction. Offers book catalog (send for it with business-size envelope and 1 first-class stamp). Does not accept unsolicited MSS.

KELSEY ST. PRESS

P.O. Box 9235
Berkeley, CA 94709
(510) 845-2260
Fax: (510) 548-9185
E-mail: kelseyst@sirius.com
World Wide Web:
http://www.sirius.com/~kelseyst/index.html
Rena Rosenwasser

Publishes lesbian fiction and poetry. Publishes 2–3 books per year. Letter of query should precede MS submissions. MSS should be sent to Patricia Dienstfrey. Accepts MSS not represented by agents. Reads unsolicited MSS only in the months of June and July. Accepts simultaneous submissions. Returns MSS with SASE. Marketing budget depends on grants received. Has a per-book marketing budget of $300. Pays royalties. Tips: "Our interest is in experimental work by women that explores voice and language. We also publish collaborations between writers and artists."

LAUGHLINES PRESS*

P.O. Box 259
Bala Cynwyd, PA 19004
(610) 668-4252
Orders Only: (800) 356-9315
E-mail: rozwarren@aol.com

Publishes humor books by women, with a special emphasis on cartoon collections and lesbian humor. Publishes 3–4 books per year. Responds to MS and query submissions in 1 week. Accepts MSS not represented by agents. Accepts unsolicited MSS. Accepts MSS that are simultaneous submissions. Returns MSS with SASE. MSS should be typed, double-spaced. Pays standard royalty.

LIBRA PUBLISHERS, INC.

3089C Clairmont Drive, Suite 383
San Diego, CA 92117
(619) 571-1414
William Kroll

Publishes lesbian and gay fiction, nonfiction, poetry, erotica, news, academic, historical, religious, and spirituality subjects. Receives 2,000 MS and query submissions per year. Publishes 8–15 books per year. Offers book catalog (send for it with 10 x 13 envelope and $1.50 in postage). Letter of query (with SASE) should precede MS submission. Responds to queries in 1 week. Responds to MS submissions in 1–3 weeks. Accepts MSS not represented by agents. Accepts unsolicited MSS. Accepts MSS that are simultaneous submissions. Returns MSS with SASE. Pays royalties.

LITTLE, BROWN AND COMPANY/CHILDREN'S BOOKS*
34 Beacon Street
Boston, MA 02108
(617) 227-0730
Fax: (617) 227-8344
Erica Stahler

Publishes general/children's books. Publishes 60 books per year. Receives approximately 6,000 MS and query submissions per year. Letter of query (with SASE) should precede MS submission. Responds to queries in 1–2 months. Responds to MS submissions in 3–4 months. Does not accept MSS not represented by agents. Does not accept unsolicited MSS. Accepts MSS that are simultaneous submissions. Returns MSS with SASE. MSS should be typed, double-spaced. MSS for picture books should be 1,000–1,500 words; young adult novels 25,000–35,000 words; middle grade novels 15,000–25,000 words. Pays royalties against advance.

MADWOMAN PRESS
P.O. Box 690
Northboro, MA 01532
(508) 393-3447
Diane Benison

Publishes lesbian fiction, nonfiction, and cartoons and comics. Publishes 1–2 books per year. Letter of query (with SASE) should precede MS submission. Responds to queries within 8 weeks. Responds to MS submissions within 16 weeks. Accepts MSS not represented by agents. Accepts MSS that are simultaneous submissions. Returns MSS with SASE. MSS of approximately 52,000 words or 200 pages of about 250 words per page preferred. MSS should be typed, double-spaced. Dot-matrix submissions accepted. Pays royalties. Tips: "We publish books by, for, and about lesbians and are especially interested in mysteries, spy novels, cartoons, and comics.

MAISONNEUVE PRESS*
P.O. Box 2980
Washington, DC 20013-2980
(301) 277-7505
Fax: (301) 277-2467
E-mail: rmerril@mica.edu

Publishes lesbian and gay academic and historical subjects. Offers MS guidelines (free on request). Publishes 4–8 books per year. Has an annual overall marketing budget of $10,000. Receives 400 MS and query submissions per year. Letter of query (with SASE) should precede MS submission. Responds to queries in 1 month. Responds to MS submissions in 4 months. Accepts MSS not represented by agents. Accepts unsolicited MSS. Accepts MSS that are simultaneous submissions. Returns MSS. MSS should be 225–275 pages, but will consider MSS of other lengths. Pays royalties.

MANHOOD RITUALS*
P.O. Box 14695
San Francisco, CA 94114
(415) 864-3456
Fax: (415) 282-3492
John H. Embry

Publishes gay male leather and SM erotica. Offers MS guidelines. Prefers computer disk submissions. Responds to queries in 2 weeks. Responds to MS submissions in 30 days. Pays on publication. Tips: "Leather erotica with no legal ramifications."

MASQUERADE BOOKS*
801 Second Avenue
New York, NY 10017
(212) 661-7878
Fax: (212) 986-7355
E-mail: masqbks@aol.com

Publishes lesbian and gay fiction, nonfiction, and erotica. Offers MS guidelines (send for them with SASE). Publishes 180 books per year. Letter of query (with SASE) should precede MS submission. Accepts MSS not represented by agents. Accepts unsolicited MSS. Accepts MSS that are simultaneous submissions. Returns MSS.

MENTOR PRESS*
8571-B Sudley Road
Manassas, VA 20110
(703) 330-5600
Fax: (703) 330-8357
E-mail: bruce@pubpartners.com
World Wide Web: http://www.pubpartners.com

Publishes gay male fiction, nonfiction, religious, historical, and spirituality subjects. Offers MS guidelines (send for them with SASE). Has an annual overall marketing budget of $10,000. Letter of query (with SASE) should precede MS submission. Responds to queries in 30 days. Responds to MS submissions in 6 weeks. Accepts MSS not represented by agents. Does not accept unsolicited MSS. Accepts MSS that are simultaneous submissions. Returns MSS with SASE. MSS should be typed, double-spaced. Pays royalties. Tips: "Always query first with proposal, sample chapters, and clips."

MONUMENT PRESS*
P.O. Box 140361
Irving, TX 75014-0361
(972) 686-5332
Rick Donovon

Publishes lesbian and gay academic and historical subjects. Offers MS guidelines (send for them with SASE). Publishes 20 books per year. Has an annual overall marketing budget of $200,000. Receives 1,000 MS and query submissions per year. Letter of query (with SASE) should precede MS submission. Responds to MS and query submissions in 4–5 months. Accepts MSS not represented by agents. Does not accept unsolicited MSS. Does not accept MSS that are simultaneous submissions. Returns MSS with SASE. Pays royalties.

NAIAD PRESS, INC.
P.O. Box 10543
Tallahassee, FL 32302
(904) 539-5965
Fax: (904) 539-9731
Barbara Grier

Publishes lesbian fiction, nonfiction, erotica, academic, and historical subjects. Offers MS guidelines (send for them with business-size envelope and 2 first-class stamps). Receives 1,500 MS and query submissions per year. Publishes 28 books per year. Offers book catalog (free on request). Letter of query (with SASE) must precede MS submission. Accepts MSS not represented by agents. Does not accept MSS that are simultaneous submissions. Returns MSS with SASE. Fiction MSS should be no longer than 50,000 words. Responds to MS submissions in 3–6 months. MSS should be $8^1/_2$ x 11, white paper, typed, double-spaced, consecutively-numbered pages. $1^1/_2$-inch top and bottom margins. $1^1/_4$-inch side margins. No more than 25 lines to a page. Dot-matrix submissions accepted. Has an average annual overall marketing budget

44

of $200,000. Has an average per-book marketing budget of $8,000–$10,000. Pays royalties. Tips: "You are competing in a market where for every book published in this fast growing sub-field, at least 250 exist that are as good or better that don't get accepted. Serve yourself. Write to the publisher and get explicit guidelines about how to submit to that publisher. Read their works and be sure you understand what they are looking for. Be sure your book is done—finished to the best of your ability—when you first send it in. Never send queries or manuscripts to more than one publisher at a time. The best won't compete, so don't mandate rejection before you begin. Go to the library and get a manuscript preparation manual and make sure what you send in looks very good."

NATIONAL ASSOCIATION OF SOCIAL WORKERS
The NASW Press
750 First St, N.E., Suite 700
Washington, DC 20002
(202) 336-8214
Linda Beebe

Publishes books and scholarly journals for professional and social workers on a wide variety of topics. Invites gay and lesbian submissions. Offers MS guidelines (free on request). Receives over 1,000 MS and query submissions per year. Publishes 12–20 books per year. Offers book catalog (free on request). Responds to MS and query submissions in 3–4 months. Accepts MSS not represented by agents. Accepts unsolicited MSS. Accepts MSS that are simultaneous submissions (for books only). Journal MSS should be no longer than 20 pages. Book MSS should be no longer than 600 pages. Has an average annual overall marketing budget of $250,000 for books. Pays royalties for books accepted. Offers no payment for works published in the journals.

NEW SOCIETY PUBLISHERS
P.O. Box 189
Gabriola Island, BC V0R 1X0 Canada
(250) 247-9737
Orders: (800) 567-6772
Fax: (250) 247-7471
E-mail: nsp@island.net
World Wide Web: http://www.swifty.com/nsp/
Judith Plant

Publishes nonfiction about fundamental social change through nonviolent action. Publishes 12 books per year. Offers book catalog (free on request). Letter of query (with SASE) should precede MS submission. Accepts MSS not represented by agents. Accepts MSS that are simultaneous submissions. Returns MSS with SASE. MSS should be no longer than 280 pages. MSS should be typed, double-spaced. Has an average annual overall marketing budget of $6,600. Pays royalty advance (half on contract signing, half on receipt of final MS), plus 10% net royalties after expenses. Tips: "Do your homework. Find out if the publishing house does the kind of work you're proposing, then find out what process they use and follow it."

NEW VICTORIA PUBLISHERS
P.O. Box 27
Norwich, VT 05055
(802) 649-5297
Fax: (802) 649-5297
E-mail: newvic@aol.com
World Wide Web:
http://www.opendoor.com/NewVic/

Publishes lesbian fiction. Also considers nonfiction, particularly history and biography. Offers MS guidelines (send for them with business-size envelope and 1 first-class stamp). Receives 150–200 MS and query submissions per year. Publishes 8 books per year. Offers book catalog (free on request). Letter of query (with SASE) should precede MS submission. Responds to queries in 2 weeks.

Responds to MS submissions in 1 month. Accepts MSS not represented by agents. Accepts unsolicited MSS. Prefers not to receive MSS that are simultaneous submissions. Pays royalties. Tips: "If you want a response, always send a SASE. We like well-written material with strong characterization. A bit of humor helps as well."

NEW YORK UNIVERSITY PRESS
P.O. Box 1235
New York, NY 10008-1235
E-mail: jay@pace.edu
Karla Jay

Publishes lesbian nonfiction, political, social sciences, miscellaneous academic, historical, religious, literary, and spirituality subjects in *The Cutting Edge: Lesbian Life and Literature* series. No memoirs, monographs, or contemporary fiction. Offers MS guidelines only after acceptance of MS. Receives over 50 MS and query submissions per year. Publishes 2–4 books per year. Letter of query should precede MS submission. Responds to queries in 2–4 weeks. Responds to MS submissions in 2–4 months. Accepts MSS not represented by agents. Does not accept unsolicited MSS. Returns MSS with SASE. MSS should be typed, double-spaced. Letter-quality preferred. Payment varies. Tips: "Writers need to be clear about goals for the manuscript; whom it is intended for; when revisions can be made, etc."

NORTHEASTERN UNIVERSITY PRESS
360 Huntington Avenue
Boston, MA 02115
(617) 373-5480
Fax: (617) 373-5483
Jill Bahcall

Publishes women's studies and feminist nonfiction, American history, ethnic literature, music, and criminal justic subjects. Receives approximately 250 MS and query submissions per year. Publishes approximately 40 books per year. Offers book catalog (free on request). Letter of query should precede MS submission. Responds to queries in approximately 2 months. Responds to MS submissions in approximately 4 months. Accepts MSS not represented by agents. Accepts unsolicited MSS. Accepts MSS that are simultaneous submissions, but author should so notify. Returns MSS with SASE. MSS should be typed, double-spaced. Letter-quality submissions preferred. Pays royalties.

OBELESK BOOKS/TRIANGLE TITLES*
P.O. Box 1118
Elkton, MD 21922-1118
(410) 392-3640
E-mail: obelesk@netgsi.com
Gary Bowen

Publishes gay, lesbian, and multicultural science fiction, fantasy, and horror. Offers MS guidelines (send for them with SASE). Publishes 2 books per year. Receives 400 MS and query submissions per year. Letter of query (with SASE) should precede MS submission. Responds to MS and query submissions in 2–4 weeks. Accepts MSS not represented by agents. Accepts unsolicited MSS. Accepts MSS that are simultaneous submissions. MSS should be 1,000–5,000 words. MSS should be typed, double-spaced. Pays flat fee on publication.

THE OUTBOUND PRESS
89 Fifth Avenue, Suite 803
New York, NY 10003
(212) 727-2751

Publishes gay male erotica. Offers MS guidelines (send for them with SASE). Responds to

MS and query submissions in 3 weeks. Accepts MSS not represented by agents. Accepts unsolicited MSS. Does not accept MSS that are simultaneous submissions. Returns MSS with SASE. Offers advances and royalties. Also publishes *Bondage Recruits, Bound & Gagged,* and *Pledges & Paddles.* See listings in "Magazines & Journals" section. Tips: "Interests are directed toward cutting-edge books with focus specifically directed towards bondage and SM between men."

OXFORD UNIVERSITY PRESS
198 Madison Avenue
New York, NY 10016
(212) 726-6000

A mainstream publishing house that publishes lesbian and gay nonfiction, academic, and historical subjects. Publishes 1,200 books per year (300 in U.S. office). Offers book catalog. Letter of query (with SASE) should precede MS submission. Responds to queries in 1 month. Accepts MSS not represented by agents. Accepts unsolicited MSS. Accepts MSS that are simultaneous submissions. Returns MSS with SASE. Offers standard advances for trade books; often pays net royalties. Tips: "We are an academic publisher. Most of our authors teach or have taught at the university level."

PAPIER-MACHÉ PRESS
135 Aviation Way #14
Watsonville, CA 95076
(408) 763-1420
Fax: (408) 763-1421
Shirley Coe

Publishes feminist fiction and nonfiction. Offers MS guidelines (send for them with business-size envelope and 1 first-class stamp). Publishes 8 books per year. Receives 3,000–4,000 MS and query submissions per year. Letter of query (with SASE) should precede MS

submission. Responds to queries in 2–3 months. Responds to MS submissions in 3–4 months. Accepts MSS not represented by agents. Accepts MSS that are simultaneous submissions. Returns MSS with SASE. Short story and novel MSS should be a minimum of 200 pages. Pays advances and royalties. Tips: "We publish books for midlife and older women that present important social issues. We seek diversity in the perspectives presented, especially in our theme anthologies."

PERIWINKLE BOOKS*
Box 8052
Victoria, British Columbia V8W 3R7 Canada
(250) 382-5868
E-mail: hannah@islandnet.com
Tanya Yaremchuk

Publishes lesbian and gay fiction, erotica, poetry, and youth subjects. Offers MS guidelines (send for them with SASE). Publishes 5–6 books per year. Receives 150–200 MS and query submissions per year. Responds to queries in 1 month. Responds to MS submissions in 3–6 months. Accepts MSS not represented by agents. Accepts unsolicited MSS. Does not accept MSS that are simultaneous submissions. Returns MSS with SASE. MSS should be typed, double-spaced, paginated, with author's name on each page. Pays small advance and royalties.

PERMEABLE PRESS
47 Noe Street #4
San Francisco, CA 94114
World Wide Web: http://www.permeable.com
Brian Clark

Publishes lesbian and gay fiction, nonfiction, erotica, news, historical, religious, spirituality subjects, and radical politics. Offers MS guidelines (send for them with business-size envelope and 1 first-class stamp). Publishes 4–8 books per year. Offers book catalog (send for it with business-size envelope and 1 first-class stamp). Letter of query should include SASE. Responds to queries in 2 weeks to 2 months. Reponds to MS submissions in 1–2 months. Accepts MSS not represented by agents. Accepts unsolicited MSS. Accepts MSS that are simultaneous submissions. Returns MSS with SASE. MSS should be typed, double-spaced. Prefers letter-quality submissions. Has an average annual marketing budget of $100,000. Has an average per-book marketing budget of $7,500. Pays royalties.

THE PILGRIM PRESS
700 Prospect E., 4th Floor
Cleveland, OH 44115-1100
(216) 736-3725
Fax: (216) 736-3703
E-mail: stavet@ucc.org
Timothy G. Staveteig

Publishes lesbian and gay nonfiction, religious, and spirituality subjects. Offers MS guidelines (send for them with business-size envelope and 1 first-class stamp). Publishes 5 books per year. Offers book catalog (free on request). Letter of query (with SASE) should precede MS submission. Responds to queries promptly. Accepts unsolicited MSS. Accepts MSS not represented by agents. Returns MSS with SASE. Pays royalties.

THE POST-APOLLO PRESS
35 Marie Street
Sausalito, CA 94965
(415) 332-1458
Fax: (415) 332-8045
E-mail: tpapress@dnai.com
Simone Fattal

Publishes fiction, lesbian fiction, poetry, and nonfiction spirituality subjects. Publishes 2 books per year. Offers book catalog (send for it with business-size envelope and 1 first-class stamp). Responds to MS and query submissions in 3 months. Accepts MSS not represented by

agents. Accepts unsolicited MSS. Does not accept MSS that are simultaneous submissions. Returns MSS with SASE. MSS should be typed, double-spaced. Pays royalties. Tips: "Try to be yourself."

PRESS GANG PUBLISHERS
101 225 E. 17th Avenue
Vancouver, BC V5V 1A6
(604) 876-7787
Fax: (604) 876-7892
E-mail: pgangpub@portal.ca

Publishes feminist and lesbian fiction, nonfiction, erotica, and political subjects. Receives 150–200 MS and query submissions per year. Publishes 5 books per year. Offers book catalog (free on request). Letter of query (with SASE) should precede MS submission. Responds to queries in 2 months. Responds to MS submissions in 3–4 months. Accepts MSS not represented by agents. Accepts unsolicited MSS. Accepts MSS that are simultaneous submissions. Returns MSS with SASE. MSS should be typed, double-spaced. Prefers letter-quality submissions. Pays royalties. Tips: "U.S. writers must send postal coupons—not U.S. stamps—on SASE. We give priority to Canadian women's writing. We are not soliciting poetry submissions at this time."

PROMETHEUS BOOKS PUBLISHER*
59 John Glenn Drive
Amherst, NY 14228-2197
(716) 691-0133
Fax: (716) 691-0137
E-mail: pbooks6205@aol.com
Steven L. Mitchell

Publishes lesbian and gay fiction, nonfiction, academic, and religious subjects. Publishes 70–80 books per year. Receives 2,000+ MS and query submissions per year. Letter of query (with proposal and SASE) should precede MS submission. Responds to queries in 4–6 weeks.

Responds to MS submissions in 8–10 weeks. Accepts MSS not represented by agents. Accepts unsolicited MSS. Accepts MSS that are simultaneous submissions. MSS should be typed, double-spaced.

PUBLISHERS ASSOCIATES
Box 140361
Las Colinas, TX 75014-0361
(214) 686-5332
Belinda Buxjom

Publishers Associates is a consortium of independent/academic presses, which include the Liberal Press, Liberal Arts Press, Monument Press, Minuteman Press, Scholars Books, Tangelwuld Press, Stardate 2000, Nichole Graphics, and Galaxy 5000. Belinda Buxjom is Senior Editor for the consortium. Jeff Stryker is the gender studies and gay/lesbian histories editor. Publishes lesbian and gay nonfiction, liberal politics. Priority: academic, historical, and minority subjects. Submissions must be liberal in nature and nonsexist/nongender if philosophical or sociological/psychological. Receives 400 MS and query submissions per year. Publishes 100 books per year. Book catalog available (send for it with 6 x 9 envelope and 90¢ postage). Letter of query (with SASE) should precede MS submission. Responds to MS and query submissions in 3 months. Accepts MSS not represented by agents. Accepts unsolicited MSS. Returns MSS with SASE. Minimum MS length is 50 pages. MSS should be 8¹/₂ x 11, typed, double-spaced, 1-inch margins. Dot-matrix submissions accepted. Photocopied submissions accepted. No child nudity. Has an average annual overall marketing budget of $50,000. Has an average per-book marketing budget of $5,000. Pays royalties. Tips: "Clear, concise, concrete, crisp plain English without affectation will get a contract before labored, pseudoacademic writing (big words that

require a run to the unabridged dictionary). All works must have a bibliography or a complete listing in the footnotes author's full name, full title and subtitle, city and state/province/country of publication, publisher, date, volume number (if applicable), and pagination (pages cited). No sexism. If a lesbian work, author can't degrade gay males, and vice versa. Emphasize gay and lesbian rights."

QUEER ASSOCIATED PRESS*
P.O. Box 11574
Washington, D.C. 20008
(888) 353-1904
Fax: (202) 363-5824
E-mail: queerasspr@aol.com

Publishes gay male fiction, alternative erotica, gay and lesbian parody. Receives 10–100 MS and query submissions per year. Letter of query (with SASE) should precede MS submission. Responds to queries in 3–12 weeks. Reponds to MS submissions in 3–5 months. Accepts MSS not represented by agents. Accepts unsolicited MSS. Does not accept MSS that are simultaneous submissions. Returns MSS with SASE. Submit MSS with cover letter giving address, telephone number, and e-mail address. Prefers MSS to be spiral bound. Pays on publication.

RAINBOW BOOKS, INC.*
P.O. Box 430
Highland City, FL 33846
(941) 648-4420
Fax: (914) 648-4420
Betsy Lampe

Publishes how-to/self-help, gender issues, children's books with parents who are homosexual. Offers MS guidelines (send for them with SASE). Publishes 15–20 books per year. Receives 600 MS and query submissions per year. Letter of query (with SASE) should precede

MS submission. Responds to queries in 2 weeks. Responds to MS submissions in 6–8 weeks. Accepts MSS not represented by agents. Accepts unsolicited MSS. Accepts MSS that are simultaneous submissions. Returns MSS with SASE. MSS should be typed, double-spaced. Prefers letter-quality submissions. Offers advances and pays royalties. Tips: "No sexually explicit material. Submit credentials in how-to/self-help to assist in selling nonfiction titles."

RELIEF PRESS*
P.O. Box 4033
South Hackensack, NJ 07606
(201) 641-3003
Fax: (201) 641-1253
E-mail: reliefron@aol.com
Ronnie L. Smith

Publishes lesbian nonfiction and poetry. Publishes 1 book per year. Receives 100 MS and query submissions per year. Does not accept unsolicited MSS. Tips: "At this time we are not accepting unsolicted submissions. Our small press was created as an offshoot of our successful submission service, Writer's Relief. We will continue to publish on per-project basis only."

RISING TIDE PRESS
5 Klvy Street
Huntington Station, NY 11746
(516) 427-1289
E-mail: rtpress@aol.com
Lee Boojamra

Publishes lesbian fiction (romance, science fiction, mystery, horror), nonfiction, erotica, humor, and political subjects. Offers MS guidelines (send for them with 4 x 10 envelope and 1 first-class stamp). Receives 150–200 MS and query submissions per year. Publishes 8–10 books per year. Letter of query (with SASE) should precede MS submission. Responds to

queries in 1 week. Responds to MS submissions in 2–3 months. Accepts MSS not represented by agents. Accepts unsolicited MSS. Does not accept MSS that are simultaneous submissions. Returns MSS with SASE. MSS should be typed, double-spaced. Dot-matrix submissions accepted. Letter-quality submissions preferred. Pays royalties. Tips: "Proof manuscript before submitting. Each manuscript should be neat and clean, carefully prepared."

ROUTLEDGE, INC.
29 West 35th Street
New York, NY 10023
(212) 244-3336
Mr. Germano

Publishes lesbian and gay nonfiction, academic, and historical subjects. Receives over 1,000 MS and query submissions per year. Publishes 150 books per year. Letter of query (with SASE) should precede MS submission. Accepts MSS not represented by agents. Returns MSS with SASE. MSS should be typed, double-spaced. Tips: "We specialize in scholarly books. Lesbian/gay studies is only one part of our program, but we publish extensively in cultural studies and in women's studies. Books most likely to be accepted will be either (1) scholarly works (e.g., history, cultural theory) or (2) general interest (trade) titles with a particular appeal to educated readers."

RUTGERS UNIVERSITY PRESS
Building 4161
Livingston Campus RU
New Brunswick, NJ 08903-5062
Marile Wasserman

Publishes lesbian and gay nonfiction, political, academic, historical, and religious subjects. Receives 1,000 MS and query submissions per year. Publishes 60 books per year. Offers book catalog (free on request). Letter of query should precede MS submission. Responds to queries in 1 day to 2 weeks. Responds to MS submissions in 1 day to 3 months. Accepts MSS not represented by agents. Accepts unsolicited MSS. Accepts MSS that are simultaneous submissions. Returns MSS with SASE. MSS should be a minimum of 200 pages and a maximum of 450 pages. MSS should be $8^{1}/_{2}$ x 11, typed, double-spaced. Photocopied submissions accepted. Dot-matrix submissions accepted. Pays royalties. Tips: "Be clear. Be brief. Look at our catalog before you submit."

SAGE PUBLICATIONS, INC.
2455 Teller Road
Thousand Oaks, CA 91320
(805) 499-0721 x7213
Fax: (805) 499-0871
E-mail: terry_hendrix@sagepub.com
Charles T. Hendrix

Publishes lesbian and gay scholarly nonfiction works for advanced undergraduate/graduate students, teachers, researchers in the social sciences, and practitioners, graduate students, and teachers/researchers in the helping professions (clinical psychology, counseling, social work, nursing, etc.). Offers MS guidelines (free on request). Receives 2,000–3,000 MS and query submissions per year. Publishes 200 books per year. Offers book catalog (free on request). Responds to queries in 6–8 weeks. Responds to MS submissions in 6 weeks to 3 months. Accepts MSS not represented by agents. Accepts unsolicited MSS. Accepts MSS that are simultaneous submissions (author should so state in cover letter). Returns MSS with SASE. MSS should be 200–350 pages. Prefers MSS submitted in American Psychological Association style for text and references; no footnotes; typed, double-spaced. Letter-quality submissions preferred. Has an average annual marketing budget of $3

million. Royalties paid on an annual basis. Tips: "We prefer to review a proposal and outline along with the author's vita as the first step. If the proposal seems to fit our current publishing program, we will ask to review 2 or 3 sample chapters in draft form. We have 'Guidelines for Developing a Proposal' available free upon request."

SANGUINARIA PUBLISHING
85 Ferris Street
Bridgeport, CT 06605
(203) 576-9168
Selma Miriam

The owners of a feminist bookstore and vegetarian restaurant. Published 3 political cookbooks, 1 cartoon book, and 2 series of note cards. May publish other subjects in the future. Offers book catalog. Letter of query (with SASE) should precede MS submission. Accepts MSS not represented by agents.

SCARECROW PRESS, INC.
4720 Boston Way
Lanham, MD 20706
(301) 459-3366
Shirley Lambert

Publishes lesbian and gay nonfiction reference material for the library market. Offers MS guidelines (free on request). Publishes approximately 150 books per year. Offers book catalog (free on request). Accepts MSS not represented by agents. Accepts unsolicited MSS. Occasionally accepts MSS that are simultaneous submissions; prefers exclusive right to review. Responds to MS submissions in 4–6 weeks. MSS should be a minimum of 250 pages, typed, double-spaced. Pays royalties.

THE SEAL PRESS

3131 Western Avenue, Suite 410
Seattle, WA 98121
(206) 283-7844
Fax: (206) 285-9410
E-mail: sealprss@scn.org
World Wide Web: http://www.sealpress.com
Faith Conlon, Holly Morris

Publishes feminist and lesbian nonfiction. Offers MS guidelines (send for them with business-size envelope and 1 first-class stamp). Receives 1,000 MS and query submissions per year. Publishes 15 books per year. Offers book catalog (free on request). Letter of query (with SASE) should precede MS submission. Responds to queries in 4 weeks. Responds to MS submissions in 6–8 weeks. Accepts MSS not represented by agents. Accepts unsolicited MSS. Does not accept MSS that are simultaneous submissions. Returns MSS with SASE. MSS should be $8^1/_2$ x 11, typed, double-spaced. Letter-quality submissions preferred. Pays royalties. Tips: "Familiarize yourself with potential publishers in order to evaluate whether your work would be suitable for their consideration."

SOMERSAULT PRESS

P.O. Box 1428
El Cerrito, CA 94530-1428
(510) 215-2207
Shelley Anderson

Publishes short fiction. Publishes 1 book per year. Receives 300–400 MS and query submissions per year. Responds to MS and query submissions in 3–4 weeks. Accepts MSS not represented by agents. Accepts unsolicited MSS. Accepts MSS that are simultaneous submissions. No guidelines or restrictions. $10 entry fee per envelope. No story limit. Multiple submissions encouraged but must be submitted in one envelope. Returns MSS with SASE. Pays $10 per printed page at time of publication. Prizes: $500 first prize, $200 second prize, and $100 third prize. Tips: "Looking for solid, accessible, imaginative fiction."

SOUTH END PRESS

116 St. Botolph
Boston, MA 02115
(617) 266-0629
Fax: (617) 266-1595
E-mail: sepress@aol.com
Loie Hayes

Publishes nonfiction political subjects, including gay and lesbian issues. Receives 500 MS and query submissions per year. Publishes 10–12 books per year. Offers book catalog (free on request). Responds to MS and query submissions in 8 weeks. Accepts MSS not represented by agents. Accepts unsolicited MSS. Accepts MSS that are simultaneous submissions (please specify). Returns MSS with SASE. Offers standard book contract.

SPECTRUM PRESS

3023 N. Clark Street #109
Chicago, IL 60657
(312) 281-1419
Dan Agin
E-mail: specpress@earthlink.net
World Wide Web: http://users.aol.com/specpress

Nonprint publisher. Publishes on disk and sells books through disk and e-mail worldwide. Publishes erotica, lesbian and gay fiction, nonfiction, poetry, academic, and historical subjects. Only accepts e-mail submissions and queries. Receives 1,000 MS submissions per year. Accepts MSS not represented by agents. Accepts unsolicited MSS. Accepts MSS that are simultaneous submissions. MSS should be no less than 200,000 bytes (fiction), 3,000 lines (poetry). Address poetry, erotica, and fiction to Senior Editor Kristi Springkle at specpress@earthlink.net. Address all other submissions to Managing Editor Daniel Vian at specpress@earthlink.net. Pays royalties.

SPINSTERS INK

P.O. Box 300170
Minneapolis, MN 55403
Joan Drury

Publishes feminist fiction (especially mysteries), nonfiction, political, and contemporary issues and themes. Offers MS guidelines (send for them with business-size envelope and 1 first-class stamp). Receives 500 MS and query submissions per year. Publishes 6–8 books per year. Offers book catalog (free on request). Letter of query (with SASE) should precede MS submission. Responds to MS and query submissions in 2–3 months. Accepts MSS not represented by agents. Accepts unsolicited MSS. Accepts MSS that are simultaneous submissions, if clearly labeled. MSS should be sent to Editor. MSS should be $8^{1}/_{2}$ x 11 typed, double-spaced. Negotiates contract for royalties.

STARBOOKS PRESS/WOLDT GROUP COS.

1391 6th Street
Sarasota, FL 34236
(941) 957-1281
P. J. Powers

Publishes fiction, nonfiction, poetry, and erotica (all with an erotic overtone). Receives 30–50 MS and query submissions per year. Publishes 8–12 books per year. Offers book catalog (free on request). Letter of query (with SASE) should precede MS submission. Responds to queries in 1 week. Responds to MS submissions in 2–3 months. Accepts MSS not represented by agents. Accepts unsolicited MSS. Accepts MSS that are simultaneous submissions. Returns MSS with SASE. MSS should be $8^{1}/_{2}$ x 11, typed, notebook bound or 3-hole punched. Dot-matrix submissions accepted. Photo submissions accepted. Pays royalties. Tips: "Read. Familiarize yourself with the market. Write to that market. See what makes a best-seller."

STONEWALL INN EDITIONS/ST. MARTIN'S PRESS*

175 Fifth Avenue
New York, NY 10010
(212) 674-5151
Keith Kahla

Stonewall Inn Editions is the gay/lesbian-interest imprint of St. Martin's Press. Stonewall Inn is primarily a trade paperback line that reprints books originally published by St. Martin's in cloth editions, though books are occasionally done as trade paperback originals or bought from other publishers. Stonewall Inn consists of several sub-imprints: Stonewall Inn Mysteries (gay/lesbian-themed mysteries), Stonewall Inn Classics ("classic" gay/lesbian fiction and nonfiction), Stonewall Inn Editions (literary fiction and nonfiction), and Stonewall Inn Books (a line of small hardcover gift books of photography or text). Established in 1987, Stonewall Inn is the only gay/lesbian imprint at a major trade publishing house. Approximately 800 MSS and partials received per year. Publishes 12–20 books per year. Over 100 titles currently in print. Catalog available (free on request). Accepts MSS not represented by agents. Responds to submissions in 1–2 months. MSS should be typed, double-spaced, single-sided on standard letter-size paper. Multiple submissions are acceptable. Tip: "Visit the Stonewall Inn web site, your local library or bookstore to see what kind and range of material we publish. No poetry, young adult, or children's books. Query first and query by mail. No e-mail, fax, or phone queries or submissions will be responded to."

53

TEMPLE UNIVERSITY PRESS
Broad and Oxford Streets, USB 306
Philadelphia, PA 19122
(215) 204-8787
Fax: (215) 204-4719
E-mail: bartlett@astro.ocis.temple.edu
David Bartlett

Publishes lesbian and gay nonfiction as well as books on political science, history, American studies, women's studies, photography, philosophy, law, and Latin American studies. Publishes 70 books per year. Offers book catalog (free on request). Letter of query should precede MS submission. Responds to queries in 1–2 months. Responds to MS submissions in 3 months. Accepts MSS not represented by agents. Accepts unsolicited MSS. Accepts MSS that are simultaneous submissions. MSS should be $8^1/_2$ x 11, typed, double-spaced, one side of paper. Payment negotiated.

THE LIBERAL PRESS
P.O. Box 140361
Irving, TX 75014-0361
Rick Donovoni

Publishes lesbian and gay historical and scholarly subjects only. Offers MS guidelines (send for them with business-size envelope and 2 first-class stamps). Publishes 10 books per year. Offers book catalog (send for with 6 x 9 envelope and 4 first-class stamps). Letter of query (with SASE) should precede MS submission. Responds to queries in 3 weeks. Responds to MS submissions in 3 months. Accepts MSS not represented by agents. Accepts unsolicited MSS. Does not accept MSS that are simultaneous submissions. Returns MSS with SASE. Prefers computer disk submissions ($5^1/_4$-inch). Has an average overall marketing budget of $100,000. Has an average per-book marketing budget of $6,000. Pays royalties.

THIRD SIDE PRESS, INC.
2250 W. Farragut
Chicago, IL 60625-1802
(713) 271-3029
Fax: (713) 271-0459
Midge Stocker

Publishes lesbian fiction and women's health books. Offers MS guidelines (send for them with 52¢ in postage). Publishes 3–6 books per year. Offers book catalog (free on request). Letter of query (with SASE) should precede MS submission. Responds to queries in 1–3 weeks. Responds to MS submissions in 2–6 months. Accepts MSS not represented by agents. Accepts unsolicited MSS. Accepts MSS that are simultaneous submissions. Returns MSS with SASE. MSS should be typed, double-spaced. Pays royalties. Tips: "We focus on lesbian fiction (which we define as fiction written by a lesbian and including at least one major character who is lesbian) and women's health, although we're open to other feminist nonfiction subjects. We are looking for literary lesbian novels, and we are not soliciting collections of stories. Please look at our books or at least our catalog before sending us your manuscript."

THIRD WOMAN PRESS
P.O. Box 11187
Berkeley, CA 94712-2187
(510) 525-2187
(510) 525-8236
Norma Alarcon

Publishes Chicana/Latina and Third World women/women of color fiction, nonfiction, political, academic, historical, plays, reviews, interviews, essays, and art. Offers MS guidelines (free on request). Publishes 3–4 books per year. Letter of query (with SASE) should precede MS submission. Responds to queries in 2–3 weeks. Responds to MS submissions in 6–8 weeks. Accepts MSS not represented by agents.

Does not accept unsolicited MSS. Accepts MSS that are simultaneous submissions. MSS should be 8¹/₂ x 11, typed, double-spaced. No right-justified margins. Photo submissions accepted. Pays with copies of book. Tips: "Inquire first. Our anthologies focus on specific themes (past themes include Latina sexuality, Chicana lesbians)."

THORNGATE ROAD*
Campus Box 4240, English Department
Illinois State University
Normal, IL 61790-4240
(309) 438-7705
Fax: (309) 438-5414
E-mail: jmelled@ilstu.edu
Jim Elledge

Publishes gay, lesbian, bisexual poetry, prose poetry, and cross-genre/experimental texts for the Frank O'Hara Award Chapbook Competition; prose poetry and cross-genre/experimental texts for the by-invitation-only Berdache Chapbook Series. Offers MS guidelines (send for them with business-size envelope and 1 first-class stamp). Publishes 2–3 books per year. Receives approximately 200 MS and query submissions per year. Letter of query (with SASE) must precede MS submission. Reponds to queries in 1 week. Responds to MSS submissions in 3 months after the February 1 annual deadline for the Frank O'Hara Award Chapbook Competition. Accepts MSS not represented by agents. Accepts unsolicited MSS only in the Frank O'Hara Award Chapbook Competition. Accepts MSS that are simultaneous submissions. MSS should be no more than 24 pages; 4 pages of possible front-matter (title page, dedication page, table of contents, acknowledgments page) and as many as 20 pages of text (including "section divider" pages). MSS should be typed with one poem per page. Winners of the Frank O'Hara competition receive $200 and 25 copies. Authors published in the Berdache Chapbook Series paid with 25 free copies.

TPG/THE PATRIOT GROUP*
P.O. Box 20034
Santa Barbara, CA 93120-0034
(805) 569-2443
Fax: (805) 569-1529
E-mail: sbpadl@west.net
World Wide Web: http://www.west.net/~sbpadl
Rick Mathews

Publishes gay male fiction and erotica. Offers MS guidelines (free on request). Publishes 3 books per year. Has an overall annual marketing budget of $1,000. Letter of query should precede MS submission. Accepts MSS not represented by agents. Accepts unsolicited MSS. Accepts MSS that are simultaneous submissions. Returns MSS. Pays flat fee.

UNITARIAN UNIVERSALIST ASSOCIATION/SKINNER HOUSE BOOKS*
25 Beacon Street
Boston, MA 02108
(617) 742-2100
Fax: (617) 742-7025
E-mail: kholmstr@uva.org or skinner-house@uva.org
Kristine Holmstrand

Publishes lesbian and gay nonfiction, religious, historical, and spirituality subjects. Offers MS guidelines (free on request). Publishes 10 books per year. Receives 400 MS and query submissions per year. Letter of query (with SASE) should precede MS submission. Responds to queries in 2 months. Responds to MS submissions in 6 months. Accepts MSS not represented by agents. Accepts unsolicited MSS. Accepts MSS that are simultaneous submissions. Returns MSS with SASE. MSS should be typed, double-spaced. Prefers submissions in hard copy and disk. Pays royalties. Tips: "Please indicate in your cover letter why you have chosen to send your manuscript to Skinner

House Books. Our books mainly focus on Unitarian Universalist faith and history, but also cover topics that are of interest to Unitarian Universalists, including gay/lesbian/bisexual /transgender issues, race issues, reproductive rights, and other social justice concerns."

UNIVERSITY OF CALIFORNIA PRESS

2120 Berkeley Way
Berkeley, CA 94720
(510) 642-4247

Publishes lesbian and gay nonfiction, academic, and historical subjects. Publishes 180 hardcover books per year and 85 paperback books per year. Offers book catalog (free on request). Letter of query should precede MS submission. Accepts MSS not represented by agents. Accepts unsolicited MSS. Returns MSS with SASE. Pays royalties.

UNIVERSITY OF ILLINOIS PRESS

1325 S. Oak Street
Champaign, IL 61820
(217) 244-4680
Fax: (217) 244-8082
E-mail: rwentwor@uiuc.edu
World Wide Web: http://www.press.uillinois.edu
Richard L. Wentworth

Publishes lesbian and gay nonfiction, political, psychological, academic, historical, and American religious history subjects. Scholarly press. Publishes 110 books per year. Letter of query should precede MS submission. Responds to queries in 2 weeks. Responds to MS submissions in 2–3 months. Accepts MSS not represented by agents. Accepts unsolicited MSS. Returns MSS with SASE. MSS should be $8^1/_2$ x 11, typed, double-spaced.

UNIVERSITY OF MASSACHUSETTS PRESS

P.O. Box 429
Amherst, MA 01004
(413) 545-2217
Bruce Wilcox

Publishes lesbian and gay (gender studies) nonfiction, academic, and historical subjects. Receives 600 MS and query submissions per year. Publishes 40–45 books per year. Offers book catalog (free on request). Letter of query should precede MS submission. Responds to queries in 2 weeks. Responds to MS submissions in 2–3 months. Pays royalties. Tips: "We are interested in solid, scholarly work that subjects issues of gender to critical scrutiny."

UNIVERSITY OF MINNESOTA PRESS

2037 University Avenue S.E.
Minneapolis, MN 55414
(612) 624-2516
Ms. Bakhle

Publishes lesbian and gay nonfiction of a scholarly nature. Publishes 70 books per year. Responds to MS and query submissions in 30 days if not interested, in 3–4 months after preliminary acceptance. Accepts MSS not represented by agents. Accepts unsolicited MSS. MSS should be no longer than 400 pages. MSS should be $8^1/_2$ x 11, typed, double-spaced. Photocopied submissions accepted. Pays royalties.

WHOLESM PUBLISHING*

P.O. Box 19591
Toronto, Ontario M4W 3T9 Canada
(416) 962-1040
Fax: (416) 962-1044
E-mail: editor@alternate.com
World Wide Web: http://alternate.com
Trevor Jacques

Publishes nonfiction, academic, and historical subjects. Publishes 1–2 books per year. Receives 5–10 MS and query submissions per year. Does not accept MSS not represented by agents. Does not accept unsolicited MSS. Does not accept MSS that are simultaneous submissions. Returns MSS with SASE.

WILDCAT PRESS*

8306 Wilshire Boulevard, Box 8306
Beverly Hills, CA 90211
(213) 966-2466
Fax: (213) 966-2467
E-mail: wildcatprs@aol.com
World Wide Web:http://www.gaywired.com/wildcat

Publishes lesbian and gay fiction. Offers MS guidelines (free on request). Publishes 2–4 books per year. Has an average annual overall marketing budget of $50,000. Receives 100+ MS and query submissions per year. Letter of query (with SASE) should precede MS submission. Responds to queries within 1 month. Responds to MS submissions in 2 months. Accepts MSS not represented by agents. Accepts unsolicited MSS. Accepts MSS that are simultaneous submissions. Returns MSS with SASE. MSS should be typed, double-spaced. Dot matrix submissions accepted. Tips: "Learn what your rights are as an author. Recognize that there is a lot of competition and try to find a new niche to fill. Don't be discouraged by rejections. Look for alternate routes to your goal."

WOMAN IN THE MOON PUBLICATIONS (WIM)

P.O. Box 2087
Cupertino, CA 95015-2087
(408) 279-6626
Fax: (408) 279-6636
E-mail: womaninmoon@earthlink.com

Publishes New Age gay and lesbian poetry, fiction, nonfiction, and reference books on gay and lesbian topics. Poets must take WIM Poetry test ($10 reading fee required). Receives 50–100 MS and query submissions per year. Publishes 4–6 books per year. Offers book catalog (send $4 plus 75¢ postage). Letter of query (with SASE) should precede MS submission. Responds to queries in 1 week. All MS submissions are acknowledged within 2 weeks of receipt. Reports at end of reading period (April 1–June 30). A $10 reading fee is required for all book-length or poetry MSS. Accepts MSS not represented by agents. Accepts unsolicited MSS. Accepts MSS that are simultaneous submissions. Returns MSS with SASE. MSS should be $8^1/_2$ x 11, typed, double-spaced. Has an average annual overall marketing budget of $5,000. Has an average per-book marketing budget of $700–$3,500. Pays royalties to established authors. We like to copublish prepublication editions to test market. Tips: "One should be persistent, but polite. Send track record of publications and a statement of writing/poetic philosophy. We have three poetry contests and one grant. Write for information (include SASE)."

WOMEN'S PRESS
517 College Street #302
Toronto, Ontario, Canada M6G 4A2
(416) 921-2425
Fax: (416) 921-4428
E-mail: wompress@web.net

Publishes lesbian fiction, nonfiction, political, and academic subjects. Offers MS guidelines (free on request). Receives 250 MS and query submissions per year. Publishes 8 books per year. Offers book catalog (free on request). Letter of query should precede MS submission. Responds to queries in 1–2 months. Responds to MS submissions in 3–6 months. Send fiction and nonfiction MSS to Managing Editor. Accepts MSS not represented by agents. Accepts unsolicited MSS. Accepts MSS that are simultaneous submissions. Returns MSS with SASE (IRC or Canadian postage). Prefers author to submit 50 pages or 2 chapters rather than entire MS. MSS should be typed, double-spaced. Also submit photocopy of MS. Pays royalties. Tips: "Women's Press is a feminist publishing house committed to producing material that supports and enhances the development of feminism in Canada. As a publishing house with a socialist-feminist outlook, we perceive feminism as inclusive of all women and as a movement opposed to racism in society. We will not publish material that we find to be racist or classist."

YALE UNIVERSITY PRESS
P.O. Box 209040
New Haven, CT 06520-9040
(203) 432-0960
Fax: (203) 432-2394
Charles Grench

Publishes lesbian and gay scholarly books. Offers MS guidelines (send for them with business-size envelope and 1 first-class stamp). Receives several thousand query submissions and 500 MS submissions per year. Publishes 210 books per year, including paperback reprints. Letter of query (with SASE) should precede MS submission. Responds to queries in 4 weeks. Responds to MS submissions in 8 weeks. Accepts MSS not represented by agents. Accepts unsolicited MSS. Accepts MSS that are simultaneous submissions. Returns MSS with SASE. MSS should be no longer than 400 pages. MSS should be typed, double-spaced, unjustified right margin. Letter-quality submissions preferred. Does not accept dot-matrix submissions. Double-spaced notes at end of MS (no footnotes at bottom of page). Photocopied submissions accepted. Publishes no original fiction. Publishes an annual volume of poetry in the Yale Series of Younger Poets competition, submissions for which are invited in February of each year.

Magazines & Journals

13TH MOON

Department of English
SUNY-Albany
Albany, NY 12222
(518) 442-4055
Judith Johnson

Publishes lesbian fiction, nonfiction, poetry, and academic subjects. Also publishes book reviews. Offers MS guidelines (send for them with business-size envelope and 1 first-class stamp). Receives 150 MS and query submissions per year. Accepts MSS not represented by agents. Accepts unsolicited MSS. Does not accept MSS that are simultaneous submissions. Returns MSS with SASE. MSS should be typed, double-spaced. Poetry MSS may be single-spaced. Letter-quality submissions preferred. Pays with 2 copies of publication. Tips: "We like experimental works." Subscription information: 1 double issue—$10; 2 double issues—$18; 3 double issues—$26

A&U, AMERICA'S AIDS MAGAZINE

25 Monroe Street, Suite 205
Albany, NY 12210-2743
(518) 426-9010
E-mail: mailbox@aumag.org
World Wide Web: http://www.aumag.org
David L. Waggoner

Publishes lesbian and gay fiction, nonfiction, poetry, news, academic, historical subjects as a cultural response to the AIDS crisis. Offers MS guidelines (send for them with business-size envelope and 1 first-class stamp).

Receives 3,500 MS and query submissions per year. Responds to MS and query submissions in 3 months. Accepts MSS not represented by agents. Accepts unsolicited MSS. Accepts MSS that are simultaneous submissions. Returns MSS with SASE. MSS should be typed. Dot-matrix submissions accepted. Pays with copies of publication. Tips: "Become familiar with *A&U* by subscribing to the magazine."

A LA BRAVA*

80 Sycamore Street
San Francisco, CA 94110
Jaime Cortez

Publishes queer Latino/Latina fiction, nonfiction, erotica, poetry, religious, historical, spirituality, and comics. Accepts MSS not represented by agents. Accepts unsolicited MSS. Accepts MSS that are simultaneous submissions. Returns MSS with SASE. MSS should be no more than 1,000 words. Prefers submissions on disk (MS Word for Macintosh preferred). Tips: "This is a publication that places a high premium on fun, sexiness, and Latino/Latina issues."

ACE PUBLISHING/ECHO MAGAZINE

P.O. Box 16630
Phoenix, AZ 85011-6630
(602) 266-0550
Fax: (602) 266-0773
E-mail: jeff4echo@aol.com
World Wide Web: http://www.echomag.com
Bill Orovan

Publishes lesbian and gay news and commentary.

THE ADVOCATE

6922 Hollywood Boulevard, 10th Floor
Hollywood, CA 90028
(213) 871-1225
Fax: (213) 467-0173
http://www.advocate.com

Publishes lesbian and gay nonfiction, erotica, news, political, academic, arts, and features. Offers MS guidelines (free on request). Receives 500 MS and query submissions per year. Letter of query should precede MS submission. Responds to queries in 1 month. Responds to MS submissions in 1–2 months. Accepts MSS not represented by agents. Accepts unsolicited MSS. Does not accept MSS that are simultaneous submissions. Returns MSS with SASE. MSS should be no longer than 12 pages, typed, double-spaced. Computer disk submissions accepted, though a hard copy is required with disk. Pays on publication. Subscription information: 1 year—$44.97; 2 years—$79.97

ADVOCATE MEN

Box 4356
Los Angeles, CA 90078-4356
(213) 871-1225
Fax: (213) 467-6805
E-mail: jerich@advocate.com
Fred Goss

Publishes gay male erotic fiction. Offers MS guidelines (send for them with business-size envelope and 1 first-class stamp). Receives 400 MS and query submissions per year. Responds to MS and query submissions in 4 weeks. MS should be no longer than 14 pages. MSS should be $8^1/_2$ x 11, typed, double-spaced. Dot-matrix submissions accepted. Buys first North American serial rights. Author retains all other rights, including reprints. Tips: "Original settings for gay male erotic fiction preferred."

AMELIA MAGAZINE

329 E Street
Bakersfield, CA 93304
(805) 323-4064
Frederick A. Raborg, Jr.

Publishes lesbian and gay fiction, nonfiction, poetry, erotica, book reviews, cartoons, illustrations, and photos. Offers MS guidelines (send for them with business-size envelope and 1 first-class stamp). Responds to MS and query submissions in 2 weeks. Accepts MSS not represented by agents. Accepts unsolicited MSS. Accepts MSS that are simultaneous submissions. Returns MSS with SASE. Fiction MSS should be no longer than 5,000 words. Poetry MSS should be no longer than 100 lines. MSS should be typed, double-spaced. Letter-quality submissions preferred. Dot-matrix submissions accepted. Pays on acceptance, except for illustrations, which are paid for on publication. Pays on acceptance for male nude illustrations accepted when frontal nudity is involved, also for photographs, for which model releases are required. Tips: "We have no taboos except for overt salaciousness. Above all, and particularly in the gay area, we look for honesty and freshness of insight. We look for maturity. In cartoons and illustrations frontal nudity is fine but no erections. We appreciate excellent drawing and anatomy."

AMERICAN BEAR*

P.O. Box 7083
Louisville, KY 40257-7083
(502) 894-8573
E-mail: amabear@ntr.net
World Wide Web: http://www.amabear.com

Publishes gay male fiction, nonfiction, erotica, and news. Offers MS guidelines (free on request).

THE AMERICAN VOICE
332 West Broadway, Suite 1215
Louisville, KY 40202
(502) 562-0045
Frederick Smock

Publishes lesbian fiction, nonfiction, and poetry. Receives 5,000 MS and query submissions per year. Responds to queries in 1 week. Responds to MS submissions in 2–3 weeks. Accepts MSS not represented by agents. Accepts unsolicited MSS. Does not accept MSS that are simultaneous submissions. Returns MSS with SASE. Pays on publication.

ART:MAG
P.O. Box 70896
Las Vegas, NV 89170
(702) 734-8121
Peter Magliocco

Does not concentrate on lesbian and gay subjects, but welcomes submissions from lesbian and gay writers. Publishes fiction and poetry. Offers MS guidelines (send for them with business-size envelope and 1 first-class stamp). Receives more than 100 MS and query submissions per year. Responds to queries in 1 month or less. Responds to MS submissions in 3 months or less. Accepts MSS not represented by agents. Accepts unsolicited MSS. Accepts MSS that are simultaneous submissions. Returns MSS with SASE. Fiction MSS should be no longer than 4,000 words. Pays with copies of publication. Tips: "Be familiar with the small press and little magazines." Subscription information: 4 issues—$10 ; Sample—$3.50

ARTS ON THE PARK, INC./ONIONHEAD
115 N. Kentucky Avenue
Lakeland, FL 33801-5044
(813) 680-2787
Dot Davis

Publishes lesbian and gay fiction and poetry. Offers MSS guidelines (send for them with business-size envelope and 1 first-class stamp). Receives 400 MS and query submissions per year. Responds to MS submissions in 8 weeks. Accepts MSS not represented by agents. Accepts unsolicited MSS. Does not accept MSS that are simultaneous submissions. Returns MSS with SASE. Fiction MS should be no longer than 4,000 words. Poetry MSS no longer than 60 lines. MSS should be typed, double-spaced. Pays with 1 copy of publication.

ATLANTIS: A WOMEN'S STUDIES JOURNAL
Mount St. Vincent University
Halifax, Nova Scotia, Canada B3M 2J6
Fax: (902) 443-1352
E-mail: Atlantis@MSVU.ca
World Wide Web: http://www.MSVU.ca/atlantis
Marilyn Porter, Christine St. Peter

Primarily publishes blind peer-academic women's studies material, including material on lesbian studies, in both theme issue and general issue formats. Also publishes some unsolicited book and film reviews, poetry, short stories, and graphic work. Offers MS guidelines (free on request). Receives 200 MS inquiries and query submissions per year. Responds to queries in 4–6 weeks. Acknowledges MS submissions in 2 weeks; 12–16 weeks before giving word of acceptance or rejection. Accepts MSS not represented by agents. Accepts unsolicited MSS. Does not return MSS unless requested and with SASE (Canadian postage or IRC attached). Does not accept MSS that are simultaneous submissions. Offers 1 copy payment for articles; tear sheets for creative materials.

B PUBLICATIONS/OH *
P.O. Box 41030
5134 Cordova Bay Road
Victoria, British Columbia V84 2K0 Canada
(800) 874-9088
Fax: (250) 658-2954
Hope

Publishes lesbian autobiography, humor, coming of age in comics. Responds to MS and query submissions in 2–6 weeks. Accepts MSS not represented by agents. Accepts unsolicited MSS. Does not accept MSS that are simultaneous submissions. Returns MSS with SASE. Gives preferences to submissions from women artists and a 3–4 page storyline, but does accept single-panel cartoons. Page storylines in black and white only. Tips: "We look for stories that speak from the heart or from experience. Fiction that offers its characters some basis in reality, which, in turn, provides an anchor for the reader to stay."

BAD ATTITUDE, INC.
P.O. Box 390110
Cambridge, MA 02139
(617) 395-4849
World Wide Web: http://www.lifestyle.com/lesbian/
Jasmine Sterling

Publishes fiction, nonfiction, and poetry concerning lesbian sexuality or erotica. Receives 200–500 MS and query submissions per year. Responds to MS and query submissions immediately. Accepts MSS not represented by agents. Accepts unsolicited MSS. Accepts MSS that are simultaneous submissions. Pays with 2 issues of publication. Tips: "Writers should draw on their own experiences."

BEAU
P.O. Box 470
Port Chester, NY 10573
Diana Sheridan
E-mail: dianaeditor@aol.com

Publishes gay male erotic fiction and nonfiction. Offers MS guidelines (free on request). Responds to MS and query submissions in 3 weeks. Accepts MSS not represented by agents. Accepts unsolicited MSS. Does not accept MSS that are simultaneous submissions. MSS should be 2,000–3,000 words. Dot-matrix submissions accepted. Pays on publication. Tips: "Write hot. Make it safe sex or set it pre-AIDS." Subscription information: 6 issues—$14.69

BITCH: FEMINIST RESPONSE TO POP CULTURE *
3128 16th Street, Box 201
San Francisco, CA 94103
(415) 864-6671
E-mail: ljervis@sirius.com
Lisa Jervis

Publishes lesbian nonfiction, media/pop culture analysis. Responds to queries in 4–6 weeks. Responds to MS submissions in 1–2 months. Accepts MSS not represented by agents. Accepts unsolicited MSS. Accepts MSS that are simultaneous submissions. Returns MSS with SASE. Pays with 3 contributor copies. Tips: "We're looking for sharp, funny commentary on the media and pop culture."

BLACK SHEETS *
P.O. Box 31155
San Francisco, CA 94131
(415) 431-0171
Fas: (415) 431-0172
E-mail: blackb@idt.net
World Wide Web: http://www.queemet.org/BlackBooks/
Bill Brent

Publishes erotica and reviews. Offers MS guidelines (send for them with business-size envelope and 1 first-class stamp). Receives 200 MS and query submissions per year. Responds immediately to queries. Responds to MS submissions in 6 weeks. Accepts MSS not represented by agents. Accepts unsolicited MSS. Does not accept MSS that are simultaneous submissions. MSS should be no more than 3,000 words. Pays on publication. Tips: "Make it hot. Make it sexy. Make it easy on yourself by sending for guidelines."

BLK

Box 83912
Los Angeles, CA 90083-0912
(310) 410-0808
Fax: (310) 410-9250
E-mail: newsroom@blk.com
Alan Bell

Publishes lesbian and gay nonfiction, news, political, and academic subjects. Offers MS guidelines (free on request). Receives 50+ MS and query submissions per year. Responds to queries in less than 2 weeks. Responds to MS submissions in less than 4 weeks. Accepts MS not represented by agents. Accepts unsolicited MSS. Accepts MSS that are simultaneous submissions, but will not print if the work appears or is scheduled to appear in another publication. Pays on publication.

BLK PUBLISHING/BLACK LACE

Box 83912
Los Angeles, CA 90083-0912
(310) 410-0808
Fax: (310) 410-9250
E-mail: newsroom@blk.com
Alycee Lane

Publishes lesbian fiction, nonfiction, poetry, erotica, news, and political subjects. The primary focus of *Black Lace* is erotica. Offers MS

guidelines (free on request). Receives 30–50 MS and query submissions per year. Responds to queries in 1 month. Responds to MS submissions in 1–4 weeks. Accepts MSS not represented by agents. Accepts unsolicited MSS. Accepts MSS that are simultaneous submissions. Returns MSS with SASE. MSS should be typed, double-spaced. Photo and artwork submissions also accepted. Offers no payment. Subscription information: 1 year—$20; 2 years—$36

BLOOD BROTHERS*

3508 Tulane Street, NE, #C
Albuquerque, NM 87107
(505) 830-0470
Wendell Ricketts

Publishes gay male fiction, erotica, politics, and poetry (leather/fetish/SM). Responds to MS and query submissions in 30 days. Accepts MSS not represented by agents. Accepts unsolicited MSS. Does not accept MSS that are simultaneous submissions. Returns MSS with SASE. MSS should be typed, double-spaced. Submit hard copy with disk. Pays with copies of publication. Tips: "*Blood Brothers* is looking for writers who can represent something other than the middle-class gay white male perspective. Cultural criticism, good fiction with a sexy edge, and all fine writing is welcome."

BLUE JEAN MAGAZINE*

P.O. Box 90856
Rochester, NY 14609
(716) 654-5070
E-mail: bluejeanmg@aol.com

Publishes lesbian fiction, nonfiction, poetry, news, art, and photography. Offers MS guidelines (send for them with SASE). Letter of query (with SASE) should precede MS submission. Responds to queries in 60–90 days. Responds to MS submissions in 30–60 days.

Accepts MSS not represented by agents. Accepts unsolicited MSS. Accepts MSS that are simultaneous submissions. Returns MSS with SASE. MSS should be typed, double-spaced. Pays on publication. Tips: "Inclusion of clear, focused, action photographs improve the chances of your article getting published. Daring feats are ideally suited for cover story consideration. Because we are advertising-free, we cannot afford to pay teen authors and/or artists for the work we publish. We only ask for one-time publication rights. This allows you to retain ownership of your work, but grants *blue jean magazine* permission to publish your work once. A release detailing one-time publication rights will be mailed to you if we are interested in publishing your work. If you enclose a SASE we will send you a written reply. Without your SASE with proper postage we cannot provide you with a reply."

BONDAGE RECRUITS*
P.O. Box 2048
231 W. 29th Street, Suite 905
New York, NY 10116-2048
(212) 736-6896
Fax: (212) 736-0255
E-mail: bobbg@aol.com
Lee Channower

Publishes gay male erotica. Offers MS guidelines (send for them with business-size envelope and 1 first-class stamp). Responds to queries in 3 weeks. Reponds to MS submissions in 3 months. Accepts MSS not represented by agents. Accepts unsolicited MSS. Does not accept MSS that are simultaneous submissions. Returns MSS with SASE. Offers no payment. Tips: "Interests directed toward first-person experiences in male bondage and SM."

THE BOTTOM LINE
1243 N. Gene Autry, Suite 121-122
Palm Springs, CA 92262
(619) 323-0552
Fax: (619) 323-8400
J. J. Suguitan

Publishes lesbian and gay news and nonfiction.

BOUND & GAGGED
P.O. Box 2048
231 W. 29th Street, Suite 905
New York, NY 10116-2048
(212) 736-6896
Fax: (212) 736-0255
E-mail: bobbg@aol.com
Lee Channower

Publishes gay male erotica. Offers MS guidelines (send for them with SASE). Responds to queries in 3 weeks. Reponds to MS submissions in 3 months. Accepts MSS not represented by agents. Accepts unsolicited MSS. Does not accept MSS that are simultaneous submissions. Returns MSS with SASE. Offers no payment. Tips: "Interests directed toward first-person experiences in male bondage and SM."

BOY NEXT DOOR*
P.O. Box 470
Port Chester, NY 10573
Diana Sheridan
E-mail: dianaeditor@aol.com

Publishes gay male erotic fiction and nonfiction. Offers MS guidelines (free on request). Responds to MS and query submissions in 3 weeks. Accepts MSS not represented by agents. Accepts unsolicited MSS. Does not accept MSS that are simultaneous submissions. MSS should be 2,000–3,000 words. Dot-matrix submissions accepted. Pays on publication. Tips: "Write hot. Make it safe sex or set it pre-AIDS." Subscription information: 6 issues—$14.69

BRUSH CREEK MEDIA

2215-R Market Street #148
San Francisco, CA 94114
(415) 552-1506
Fax: (415)552-3244
E-mail: jwbean@brushcreek.com
World Wide Web: http://www.brushcreek.com
Joseph W. Bean

Publishes *Bear, Powerplay, International Leatherman, FQ (Foreskin Quarterly), Bunkhouse, Hombres Latinos, GBM (Gay Black Men),* and *Mach*. Publishes gay male fiction, nonfiction, and erotica. Offers MS guidelines (send for them with business-size envelope and 1 first-class stamp). Receives over 200 MSS and queries per year. Does not respond to queries about fiction, but responds to fiction and erotica submissions within 1 month. Responds to queries about features and nonfiction submissions within 3 months. Accepts MSS not represented by agents. Accepts fiction MSS. Prefers submissions in PC-readable disk form (3$\frac{1}{2}$-inch only) in ASCII, Word, DOS Text, or WordPerfect, plus hard copy. Queries for nonfiction accepted by mail, e-mail or, initially, by telephone. Pays in full while magazine is on press and sends contributor copies of magazine when subscriber copies are mailed. Tips: "Be aware of the market or readership for the title you are submitting your work to. We have no place for general gay writing or even general gay erotica. All our magazines are niche market products, serving specific types and communities. Work of interest to *Bear* will be about natural, rural-minded, simple men. Only SM/fetish/leathersex work will be of interest to *Powerplay, International Leathermen, Bunkhouse,* and *Mach*. The markets of *FQ, GBM,* and *Hombres Latinos* are obvious."

BUST*

P.O. Box 319
Ansonia Station
New York, NY 10023
(212) 691-8189
E-mail: bettybust@aol.com or bust@aol.com
World Wide Web: http://www.bust.com

Publishes lesbian academic, fiction, nonfiction, erotica, historical, and news. Offers MS guidelines (free on request). Letter of query (with SASE) should precede MS submission. Responds to MS and query submissions in 3–6 months. Accepts MSS not represented by agents. Accepts unsolicited MSS. Accepts MSS that are simultaneous submissions. Returns MSS with SASE. Tips: "Write honestly."

CALYX: A JOURNAL OF ART & LITERATURE BY WOMEN

P.O. Box B
Corvallis, OR 97339
(541) 753-9384
Fax: (541) 753-0515
E-mail: calyx@proaxis.com
Margarita Donnelly

Publishes women's fiction, nonfiction, poetry, art, and book reviews. Offers MS guidelines (send for them with business-size envelope and 1 first-class stamp). Receives 5,000–9,000 MS and query submissions per year. Publishes 2 issues per year. Responds to MS submissions within 6–12 months. Accepts MSS not represented by agents. Accepts unsolicited MSS. Willing to accept MSS that are simultaneous submissions. Pays with copies of publication and subscription. Also offers a small per-page rate when funding is available. Tips: "Be familiar with our journal. Follow our guidelines for manuscript submissions. Only submit manuscripts when we are open (in 1997: October 1– November 15; not open during the spring).

CAMP REHOBOTH, INC./LETTERS FROM CAMP REHOBOTH*

39 Baltimore Avenue
Rehoboth Beach, DE 19971
(302) 227-5620
Fax: (302) 227-5604
E-mail: camprehoboth@bdsnet.com
Steve Elkins

Publishes lesbian and gay fiction, nonfiction, poetry, historical, and news subjects.

CHERRY BOYS*

P.O. Box 470
Port Chester, NY 10573
Diana Sheridan
E-mail: dianaeditor@aol.com

Publishes gay male erotic fiction and nonfiction. Offers MS guidelines (free on request). Responds to MS and query submissions in 3 weeks. Accepts MSS not represented by agents. Accepts unsolicited MSS. Does not accept MSS that are simultaneous submissions. MSS should be 2,000–3,000 words. Dot-matrix submissions accepted. Pays on publication. Tips: "Write hot. Make it safe sex or set it pre-AIDS." Subscription information: 6 issues—$14.69

CHIRON REVIEW*

522 E. South Avenue
St. John, KS 67576-2212
(316) 549-3933
E-mail: mshauers@midusa.net (put "michael" in subject box)
Michael Hathaway

Publishes lesbian and gay fiction and poetry. Offers MS guidelines (send for them with business-size envelope and 1 first-class stamp). Receives 2,400 MS and query submissions per year. Responds to MS and query submissions in 2–4 weeks. Accepts MSS not represented by agents. Accepts unsolicited MSS.

Does not accept MSS that are simultaneous submissions. Returns MSS with SASE. Pays with copies of publication. Tips: "See sample copies of literary magazines before submitting."

CIRCLES*

1705 Fourteenth Street
Boulder, CO 80302
(303) 417-1385
Fax: (303) 417-1453
Kit McChesney

Publishes lesbian nonfiction, historical, spirituality, and news. Offers MS guidelines. Responds to MS and query submissions in 4 weeks. Accepts MSS not represented by agents. Accepts unsolicited MSS. Does not accept MSS that are simultaneous submissions. MSS should be 1,500-2,000 words. MSS should be typed, double-spaced. Prefers submissions on computer disk. Pays with subscription. Tips: "*Circles is* a magazine focusing on lesbians living in Colorado. Our articles are written primarily by Colorado writers, but we do accept outside submissions."

CLAMOUR*

206 Capp Street
San Francisco, CA 94110
(415) 558-8836
Renee Gladman

Publishes lesbian fiction, nonfiction, poetry, and historical subjects. Responds to MS submissions in 1–2 months. Accepts MSS not represented by agents. Accepts unsolicited MSS. Accepts MSS that are simultaneous submissions. Returns MSS with SASE. MSS should be 5 or more pages. Pays with copies of publication. Tips: "It is important when sending out work that you are aware of what kind of work an editor or publisher is interested in, so as to save time and frustration from unnecessary rejections."

CLIO'S PSYCHE: UNDERSTANDING THE WAY OF HISTORY*
627 Dakota Trail
Franklin Lakes, NJ 07417
Paul H. Elovitz, Ph.D.

Publishes psychohistory, academic, historical, news, psychology subjects. Offers MS guidelines (send for them with business-size envelope and 1 first-class stamp). Receives 50–60 MS and query submissions per year. Letter of query should precede MS submission. Accepts MSS not represented by agents. Accepts unsolicited MSS. Does not accept MSS that are simultaneous submissions. Returns MSS with SASE. MSS should be 300–1,200 words. Offers no payment.

THE COLOURS ORGANIZATION, INC./COLOURS MAGAZINE*
1108 Locust Street, 1st Floor
Philadelphia, PA 19107
(215) 629-1852
Fax: (215) 629-1856
E-mail: colours@critpath.org

Publishes lesbian and gay academic, fiction, nonfiction, erotica, poetry, religious, historical, spirituality, fashion, and news.

COMING OUT*
P.O. Box 470
Port Chester, NY 10573
Diana Sheridan

Publishes gay male erotic fiction and nonfiction. Offers MS guidelines (free on request). Responds to MS and query submissions in 3 weeks. Accepts MSS not represented by agents. Accepts unsolicited MSS. Does not accept MSS that are simultaneous submissions. MSS should be 2,000–3,000 words. Dot-matrix submissions accepted. Pays on publication. Tips: "Write

hot. Make it safe sex or set it pre-AIDS." Subscription information: 6 issues—$14.69

CRAZY QUILT QUARTERLY
P.O. Box 632729
San Diego, CA 92163-2729
(619) 688-1023
Fax: (619) 688-1753
Jim Kitchen

Does not concentrate on lesbian and gay subjects but welcomes submissions from lesbian and gay writers. Publishes fiction, nonfiction, poetry, one-act plays, and black-and-white artwork. Offers MS guidelines. Receives 600–700 MS and query submissions per year. Responds to fiction MSS and query submissions in 3 days; poetry MS and queries in 4 weeks; plays and artwork in 3 days. Accepts MSS not represented by agents. Accepts unsolicited MSS. Accepts MSS that are simultaneous submissions. Returns MSS with SASE. MSS should be typed, double-spaced, with name on each page. Poems should be typed one to a page. Computer disk submissions accepted (WordPerfect 5.1/6.0). Pays with 2 copies of publication. Tips: "For fiction: strong characters. Don't overuse adjectives/adverbs. For poetry: poems should have universal quality. We get too many sophomoric, self-pitying 'love' pieces and poems of despair." Subscription information: 1 year—$19; 2 years—$33; Sample—$10 (current) $8 (back issues)

CREATIVE DESIGN SERVICES/LADYLIKE*
P.O. Box 61263
King of Prussia, PA 19406-1263
(610) 640-9449
Fax: (610) 648-0257
World Wide Web: http://www.cdspub.com

Publishes gay, lesbian, and transgender fiction, nonfiction, historical, humor, and news. Letter of query (with SASE) should precede MS submissions. Responds to MS and query submissions in 1–2 weeks. Accepts MSS not represented by agents. Accepts unsolicited MSS. Does not accept MSS that are simultaneous submissions. MSS should be typed, double-spaced; prefers disk submissions (ASCII). Letter-quality preferred. Single payment for one time rights.

CRONE CHRONICLES*
P.O. Box 81
Kelly, WI 83011
(307) 733-5409
E-mail: akcrone@aol.com
World Wide Web:http://www.feminist.com/crone.htm
Ann Kreilkamp

Publishes lesbian and gay nonfiction, poetry, and personal experience. Offers MSS guidelines (send for them with SASE). Receives approximately 200 MS and query submissions per year. Responds to queries in 2 weeks. Responds to MS submissions in 1–3 months. Accepts MSS not represented by agents. Accepts unsolicited MSS. Does not accept MSS that are simultaneous submissions. Returns MSS with SASE. MSS should be typed, if possible. Pays with copy of publication. Tips: "Tell us what's really going on within you."

CROSS TALK*
P.O. Box 944
Woodland Hills, CA 91365-0944
(818) 907-3053
E-mail: kymmer@xconn.com
Kymberleigh Richards

Publishes gay, lesbian, and transgender nonfiction, historical, news, and commentary. Offers MSS guidelines (send for them with business-size envelope and 1 first-class stamp). Receives 12–15 MS and query submissions per year.

Letter of query should precede MS submission. Responds to queries within a few days. Responds to MS submissions in 1–2 weeks. Accepts MSS not represented by agents. Does not accept unsolicited MSS. Accepts MSS that are simultaneous submissions. Prefers letter-quality submissions. Accepts disk submissions (ASCII text). Pays with copies of publication. Tips: "Write about subjects that interest you. Include as much information as you have access to: better to have to remove excess later than to be asked to add content you might not have."

CRUISE MAGAZINE
660 Livernois
Ferndale, MI 48220
(810) 545-9040
Fax: (810) 545-1073
Phillip O'Jibway

Publishes lesbian and gay news. Receives 12–15 MS and query submissions per year. Responds to MS and query submissions in 30 days. Accepts MSS not represented by agents. Accepts unsolicited MSS. Accepts MSS that are simultaneous submissions (requires an exclusive for local market area). Returns MSS with SASE. MSS should be 3–5 pages. MSS should be typed, double-spaced with indication of price for one-time publication. Dot-matrix submissions accepted. Pays on publication.

CRUISIN!
P.O. Box 12597
Ft. Pierce, FL 34979-2597
(561) 464-5447
Herman Nietzche

Publishes gay male art, fiction, nonfiction, poetry, and erotica. Offers MS guidelines (send for them with business-size envelope and 1 first-class stamp). Receives more than 1,000 MS and query submissions per year. Responds to MS submissions in 30 days. Accepts MSS not represented by agents. Accepts unsolicited MSS. Does not accept MSS that are simultaneous submissions. Returns MSS with SASE. MSS should be 2,500–3,000 words. MSS should be typed, double-spaced. Pays on publication.

CURVE MAGAZINE
(FORMERLY DENEUVE)
One Haight Street, Suite B
San Francisco, CA 94102
(415) 863-6538
Fax: (415) 863-1609
E-mail: CurveMag@aol.com
Shannon Turner

A lesbian lifestyle magazine that publishes arts, entertainment, news, travel, and political subjects. Does not publish fiction, poetry, or unsolicited first-person commentary. Offers submission guidelines (send for them with business-size envelope and 1 first-class stamp). Receives 400 submissions and queries per year. Responds to queries within 6 weeks; responds to submissions within 8 weeks. Accepts articles not represented by agents and unsolicited articles. Submissions will not be returned, and should be no longer than 1,500 words if unsolicited. Preferred method of submission is MS Word/Macintosh disk. Letter-quality submissions also accepted. Payment is 10 cents a word. Tips: "Writing voice is key—we look for pieces with personality and attitude. Try to include interviews, analysis, and at least three sources. Submissions may address any topic relevant to lesbians. (Stories by and about African-American lesbians particularly encouraged.) For additional tips, please see "Getting Published in Queer Magazines" by Curve editor Shannon Turner, page 21."

DRUMMER MAGAZINE
P.O. Box 410390
San Francisco, CA 94141-0390
(415) 252-1195
Wickie Stamps

Publishes gay male erotica. Offers MS guidelines (send for them with business-size envelope and 1 first-class stamp). Receives 300 MS and query submissions per year. Responds to queries in 4–6 weeks. Accepts MSS not represented by agents. Accepts unsolicited MSS. Does not accept MSS that are simultaneous submissions. Returns MSS with SASE. MSS should be typed, double-spaced. MSS should be 1,500–5,000 words. Computer disk submissions accepted. Pays on publication.

DYKE REVIEW
584 Castro Street, Suite 456
San Francisco, CA 94114
Christie Carr

Publishes lesbian fiction, fantasy; accepts nonfiction, erotica, political, and interviews. Also, visual art, photography, illustrations, and cartooning in same categories. Receives 500 MS and query submissions per year. Responds immediately to query submissions. Responds to MS submissions in 1–2 months. Accepts MSS not represented by agents. Accepts unsolicited MSS. Accepts MSS that are simultaneous submissions. Returns MSS with SASE. MSS should be typed, double-spaced. Computer disk submissions accepted (Macintosh). Pays with 2 copies of publication. Send special requests to Senior Editor, Stefin Collins. Tips: "Dyke Review is looking for substantial interview pieces, not necessarily of well-known lesbians; conversational style (no question-and-answer formats). Include good photos. We are also interested in experimental writings and visually provocative materials. Include a brief biography about what you are doing in your current life."

EDGE MAGAZINE
6434 Santa Monica Boulevard
Los Angeles, CA 90038
(213) 962-6994
E-mail: edgemag@earthlink.net
Darren J. Roberts

Publishes gay male arts, entertainment, and current events. Receives hundreds of MS and query submissions per year. Almost all of the magazine's interviews, reviews, and features are done by the in-house editorial staff. Occasionally accepts outside nonfiction and fiction, paying upon publication. MSS should be typed, double-spaced, letter-quality, and no longer than 15 pages. Include a SASE if you want a reply (usually within 8 weeks) or your manuscript returned. Tips: "Know the magazine and its voice. We want pieces that have personality and fire."

THE ELECTRONIC GAY COMMUNITY MAGAZINE
c/o The Land of Awes Information Services
P.O. Box 16782
Wichita, KS 67216-0782
(316) 269-0913
Fax: (316) 269-4208
Modem: (316) 269-3172
E-mail: awes@awes.com
World Wide Web: http://www.awes.com
Rex Rivers

Established in 1988, the world's longest running on-line publication for the gay, lesbian, and bisexual community.

ETCETERA MAGAZINE
151 Renaissance Parkway, N.E.
Atlanta, GA 30308
(404) 525-3821
Fax: (404) 525-1908
World Wide Web: http://www.etcmag.com

Publishes lesbian and gay nonfiction, news,

and entertainment. Receives 100 MS and query submissions per year. Responds to MS and query submissions in 3–4 weeks. Pays on publication. Subscription information: 13 weeks—$23; 26 weeks—$39; 52 weeks—$65; single copy $2

THE EVERGREEN CHRONICLES
P.O. Box 8939
Minneapolis, MN 55408
(612) 823-6638
E-mail: evrgrnchron@aol.com
Jim Berg

A triannual literary journal. Publishes gay, lesbian, bisexual, and transgender fiction, poetry, plays, essays, experimental writing, and black-and-white photographs and artwork. Offers MS guidelines (send for them with business-size envelope and 1 first-class stamp). Receives 400 MS and query submissions per year. Accepts MSS not represented by agents. Accepts unsolicited MSS. Does not accept MSS that are simultaneous submissions. Responds to MS and query submissions in 2 months. Send 4 copies of work. Fiction, nonfiction, essays, or plays should be no longer than 25 pages, with a limit of 1 piece. Poetry MSS should be no longer than 10 pages or 4 poems. For artwork submit clean copies up to $8^1/_2$ x 11. Buys one time rights. Submission deadlines: Spring issue—January 1; Fall issue—July 1; Summer novella contest issue—September 30.

FAG RAG
P.O. Box 15331
Kenmore Station
Boston, MA 02215
(617) 426-8752
E. Carlotta

Publishes gay fiction, nonfiction, poetry, and erotica. Receives 150 MS and query submissions per year. Letter of query (with SASE) should precede MS submission. Responds to MS and query submissions in 3–4 weeks. Accepts MSS not represented by agents. Accepts unsolicited MSS. Does not accept MSS that are simultaneous submissions. MSS should be typed, double-spaced. Pays with 3 copies of publication. Tips: "Be aware that small presses operate quite differently from commercial presses. Check what has already been published by the press you are interested in."

FEMINIST BOOKSTORE NEWS
P.O. Box 882554
San Francisco, CA 94188
(415) 626-1556
Fax: (415) 626-8970
E-mail: fbn@fembknews.com
Carol Seajay

Publishes short reviews and announcements of feminist, lesbian, and gay literature and nonfiction; articles about the feminist, lesbian, and gay book industry. Letter of query (with SASE) should precede MS submission. Responds to queries in 4–8 weeks. Responds to MS submissions in 2 weeks (4–8 weeks if MS is received unsolicited). Returns MSS with SASE. Pays with copies of publication. Tips: "*Feminist Bookstore News* is a trade magazine for feminist bookstores. All of our articles and reviews are written for and by people working in the book trades. *Feminist Bookstore News* is an excellent and effective place to advertise lesbian and feminist books. We also rent our list of 500+ feminist, lesbian, gay, and sympathetic bookstores for $15 (on labels, in zip order) and our 'core list' of 150 feminist, lesbian, and gay stores (all in the above list) for $25." Subscription information: 1 year—$70 (add $9 for Canada delivery and $19 for overseas delivery)

FEMINIST STUDIES
Women's Studies Department
University of Maryland
College Park, MD 20742
(301) 405-7413
Fax: (301) 314-9190
E-mail: femstud@umail.umd.edu
Claire G. Moses

Publishes lesbian fiction, nonfiction, poetry, academic, and historical subjects. Offers MS guidelines (free on request). Receives over 300 MS and query submissions per year. Responds to queries in several weeks. Responds to MS submissions in 4 months. Accepts MSS not represented by agents. Accepts unsolicited MSS. Does not accept MSS that are simultaneous submissions. MSS should be no longer than 15–35 pages. MSS should be 8 1/2 x 11, typed, double-spaced. Letter-quality submissions preferred. Offers no payment. Tips: "Follow the *Chicago Manual of Style.*"

FEMINIST TEACHER
Wheaton College
Norton, MA 02766
(508) 286-3732
E-mail: Feminist_Teacher@wheatonma.edu
Paula Krebs

Multidisciplinary education magazine. Publishes lesbian/feminist academic subjects aimed at all grade levels—preschool through graduate school. Offers MS guidelines (free on request). Receives 7–10 MS and query submissions per month. Responds to queries immediately. Responds to MS submissions in 3 months. Accepts MSS not represented by agents. Accepts unsolicited MSS. Does not accept MSS that are simultaneous submissions. MSS should be no longer than 4,000 words. MSS should be typed, double-spaced. Use MLA style guide. Offers no payment. Tips: "Articles must be concerned with feminist pedagogy."

FIFTY FIFTY MAGAZINE*
2336 Market Street #20
San Francisco, CA 94114
(415) 861-8210
Fax: (415) 621-1703
E-mail: fift50mag@aol.com

Publishes gay, lesbian, and alternative arts and entertainment. Offers submission guidelines (send for them with business-size envelope and 1 first-class stamp). Receives 50–60 MS and query submissions per year. Responds to queries in 2–3 weeks. Accepts MSS not represented by agents. Accepts unsolicited MSS. Accepts MSS that are simultaneous submissions. Returns MSS with SASE. MSS should be no more than 2,000 words. MSS should be typed, double-spaced. Pays on publication.

FIRST HAND MAGAZINE
P.O. Box 1314
Teaneck, NJ 07666
(201) 836-9177
Fax: (201) 836-5055
E-mail: FirstHand3@aol.com
Bob Harris

Publishes gay male erotic fiction. Offers MS guidelines (free on request). Receives 600–1,000 MS and query submissions per year. Responds to MS and query submissions in 8 weeks. MSS should be 12–20 pages, typed, double-spaced. Does not accept dot-matrix submissions. Pays on publication or within 180 days, whichever is first.

FRESH MEN
P.O. Box 4356
Los Angeles, CA 90078-4356
(213) 871-1225
Fax: (213) 467-6805
E-mail: jerich@advocate.com
Fred Goss

Publishes gay male erotic fiction. Offers MS guidelines (send for them with business-size envelope and 1 first-class stamp). Receives over 240 MS and query submissions per year. Responds to MS and query submissions in 6 weeks. Accepts MSS not represented by agents. Accepts unsolicited MSS. Does not accept MSS that are simultaneous submissions. Returns MSS with SASE. MSS should be $8^1/_2$ x 11, typed, double-spaced. Prefers computer disk submissions (with hard copy). Pays on acceptance. Buys first North American serial rights only.

FRONTIERS NEWSMAGAZINE
P.O. Box 46367
West Hollywood, CA 90046-0637
(213) 848-2222
Monica Trasandes

Publishes gay male fiction, nonfiction, news, academic, features, and analysis. Offers MS guidelines (free on request). Receives 300 MS and query submissions per year. Letter of query should precede MS submission. Responds to queries in 2 weeks. Responds to MS submissions in 6 weeks. Accepts MSS not represented by agents. Accepts unsolicited MSS. Accepts MSS that are simultaneous submissions. Returns MSS with SASE. Prefers computer disk submissions. MSS should be typed, double-spaced. Pays 6 weeks after publication.

GAY COMMUNITY NEWS (BOSTON)*
29 Stanhope Street
Boston, MA 02116
(617) 262-6969
Fax: (617) 267-0852

Publishes lesbian and gay fiction, nonfiction, academic, erotica, and news. Responds to MS submissions in 2–3 weeks. Accepts MSS not represented by agents. Accepts unsolicited MSS. Accepts MSS that are simultaneous submissions. Pays $75 per article by agreement with the editor. Sponsors Out/Write, National Writers Conference for Gay, Lesbian, Bisexual, and Transgender Writers.

GENDER & SOCIETY
Department of Sociology
University of California Santa Barbara
Santa Barbara, CA 93110
(805) 893-7773
Fax: (805) 893-3324
E-mail: gendsoc@alishaw.ucsb.edu
Beth Schneider

Publishes lesbian political, academic (social structural), and historical subjects. Seeking articles on lesbians. Primarily interested in research and theoretical pieces. Occasionally will publish special issues. Receives 200 MS submissions per year. Responds to MS submissions in 2–3 months (often less). MSS should be sent to Margaret L. Andersen, Editor. Accepts MSS not represented by agents. Accepts unsolicited MSS. Does not accept MSS that are simultaneous submissions. Offers no payment. Tips: "I very much would like to see *Gender & Society*, an academic journal, include more pieces on lesbian lives. We are also very committed to publishing pieces written by women from diverse social locations."

GENRE MAGAZINE
7080 Hollywood Boulevard, Suite 1104
Hollywood, CA 90028
(213) 467-8300
Fax: (213) 467-8365
Richard Settles

Publishes gay nonfiction, fashion, travel, and gay life issues. Receives over 100 MS and query submissions per year. Responds to MS and query submissions in 2–4 weeks. Accepts MSS not represented by agents. Accepts unsolicited MSS. Accepts MSS that are simultaneous submissions. Does not return MSS. MSS should

be typed, double-spaced. Letter-quality submissions preferred. If material is accepted, writer must submit material on computer disk (Macintosh) or e-mail. Pays on publication. Subscription information: 1 year—$9.95

GERBIL:
A QUEER CULTURE ZINE*
P.O. Box 10692
Rochester, NY 14610
(716) 262-3966
E-mail: gerbilzine@aol.com
Tony Leuzzi, Brad Pease

Publishes gay male fiction, nonfiction, academic, poetry, and historical subjects. Receives 500 MS and query submissions per year. Responds to MS submissions in 1–3 months. Accepts MSS not represented by agents. Accepts unsolicited MSS. Does not accept MSS that are simultaneous submissions. MSS should be no more than 2,500 words. Poetry MSS should be no more than 50 lines. MSS should be typed, with name and address on each page. Pays with copies of publication. Tips: "Be honest. We get a lot of poetry about coming out or about sex. These issues are fine, but we seek other interests as well. Most of our poetry comes solicited by one of the editors. Fiction/nonfiction is always welcome, when the voice is mature and genuine."

GIRLFRIENDS MAGAZINE*
3415 Cesar Chavez #101
San Francisco, CA 94110
(415) 648-9464
Fax: (415) 648-4705
E-mail: staff@gfriends.com
World Wide Web: http://www.gfriends.com
Donna Han

Publishes lesbian culture, politics, and sexuality. Offers MS guidelines (send for them with SASE). Letter of query (with SASE) should precede MS submission. Responds to MS and query submissions in 6–8 weeks. Accepts MSS not represented by agents. Accepts unsolicited MSS. Does not accept MSS that are simultaneous submissions. Returns MSS with SASE. MSS should be typed, double-spaced. Pays prior to publication. Tips: "Read several issues of the magazine before you pitch a story. Be original, be innovative. Find a 'lesbian' story in places others wouldn't think to look."

THE GUIDE

P.O. Box 990593
Boston, MA 02199
(617) 266-8557
Fax: (617) 266-1125
E-mail: theguide@guidemag.com
World Wide Web: http://www.guidemag.com
French Wall

Publishes gay male nonfiction, political, and sexual subjects. Receives 150–250 MS and query submissions per year. Responds to queries in 1 month. Responds to MS submissions in 3 months. Accepts MSS not represented by agents. Accepts unsolicited MSS. Accepts MSS that are simultaneous submissions. Returns MSS with SASE. MSS should be no longer than 4,000 words. MSS should be typed, double-spaced, with wide margins. Prefers computer disk submissions accepted. Pays on publication. Tips: "Brevity, humor, and pro-sex stance appreciated."

GUYS MAGAZINE

P.O. Box 1314
Teaneck, NJ 07666
(201) 836-9177
Fax: (201) 836-5055
E-mail: firsthand3@aol.com
William Spencer

Publishes gay male erotic fiction. Offers MS guidelines (free on request). Receives 600-1,000

MS and query submissions per year. Responds to MS and query submissions in 6 weeks. MS should be 12–20 pages, typed, double-spaced. Does not accept dot-matrix submissions. Submissions on disk (and hard copy) preferred. Accepts e-mail submissions. Pays on acceptance.

H MAGAZINE

430 S. Broadway
Denver, CO 80203
(303) 722-5965
Fax: (303) 698-1183
E-mail: questh@aol.com
Robert J. Schlaff

Publishes entertainment guide for gays and lesbians.

HANGING LOOSE

231 Wyckoff Street
Brooklyn, NY 11217
Fax: (212) 243-7499
Ron Schreiber, Robert Hershon, Mark Pawlak, Dick Lourie

Does not concentrate on lesbian and gay subjects but welcomes submissions from lesbian and gay writers. Publishes short fiction and poetry. Responds to MS submissions in 1–4 months. Accepts MSS not represented by agents. Accepts unsolicited MSS. Does not accept MSS that are simultaneous submissions. Pays small payment upon acceptance.

THE HARVARD GAY AND LESBIAN REVIEW

P.O. Box 180300
Boston, MA 02118
(617) 421-0082
Richard Schneider, Jr.

Publishes essays, interviews, book reviews, theater and film reviews, and some poetry. Responds to queries in 1 month. Responds to MS submissions in 1–2 months. Accepts MSS not represented by agents. Accepts unsolicited MSS. Accepts MSS that are simultaneous submissions. Does not return MSS. Review MSS should be 750–1,500 words. Essay MSS should be no longer than 5,000 words. Offers no payment. Tips: "Personal memoirs are of less interest to us than literary, social, or historical analysis. No short fiction, please."

HAYDEN'S FERRY REVIEW
Arizona State University
Box 871502
Tempe, AZ 85287-1502
(602) 965-1243
E-mail: hfr@asuvm.inre.asu.edu

Does not concentrate on lesbian and gay subjects but welcomes submissions from lesbian and gay writers. Publishes fiction, nonfiction, and poetry. Offers MS guidelines (send for them with business-size envelope and 1 first-class stamp). Receives 4,000–6,000 MS and query submissions per year. Responds to queries in 1–2 weeks. Responds to MS submissions in 3–4 months. Accepts MSS not represented by agents. Accepts unsolicited MSS. Does not accept MSS that are simultaneous submissions. Returns MSS with SASE. MSS should be typed, double-spaced. Does not accept dot-matrix submissions. Pays with 2 copies of publication.

HOT SHOTS
7060 Convoy Court
San Diego, CA 92111
(619) 278-9080
Fax: (619) 278-9081
E-mail: hotshot2@ix.netcom.com
Ralph Cobar

Publishes gay male erotic fiction. Offers MS guidelines (send for them with business-size envelope and 1 first-class stamp). Receives 400 MS and query submissions per year. Letter

of query (with SASE) should precede MSS submission. Responds to queries in 3 weeks. Responds to MS submissions in 2 months. Accepts MSS not represented by agents. Accepts unsolicited MSS. Does not accept MSS that are simultaneous submissions. Returns MSS with SASE. MSS should be 2,000–2,500 words. Pays around publication date.

HUES (HEAR US EMERGING SISTERS)*
P.O. Box 7778
Ann Arbor, MI 48107
(313) 971-0023
Fax: (313) 971-0450
E-mail: hues@branson.org
World Wide Web: http://www.hues.net
Ophira Edut

Publishes lesbian, feminist, multicultural nonfiction. Offers MS guidelines (send for them with business-size envelope and 1 first-class stamp). Letter of query (with SASE) should precede MS submission. Responds to queries in 4–6 weeks. Accepts unsolicited MSS. Accepts MSS that are simultaneous submissions. Offers no payment. Tips: "Writing that is fresh, funny, hip, and down-to-earth receives preference (where applicable). Writing should also be inclusive and supportive of women of all cultures, shapes, and sexual orientations."

HURRICANE ALICE
Department of English
Rhode Island College
Providence, RI 02908
(401) 456-8377
Maureen Reddy

Publishes lesbian fiction and nonfiction. Offers MS guidelines (send for them with letter-size envelope and 1 first-class stamp). Receives 500 MS and query submissions per year. Responds to queries in 2 weeks. Responds to

MS submissions in 3 months. Accepts MSS not represented by agents. Accepts unsolicited MSS. Does not accept MSS that are simultaneous submissions or that have been published elsewhere. Returns MSS with SASE. Reviews should be no longer than 1,000 words. Fiction and nonfiction MSS should be no longer than 3,500 words. MSS should be typed, double-spaced, letter-quality. Does not accept dot-matrix submissions. Photo submissions accepted. Pays with 6 copies of publication. Tips: "Speak in a personal voice; write about things of immediate concern to you; try for as much authenticity as possible; go deeply into whatever subject you choose." Sample issue: $2.50

IRIS: A JOURNAL ABOUT WOMEN

Box 323, HSC
University of Virginia
Charlottesville, VA 22908
(804) 924-4500
Susan K. Brady

Publishes lesbian feminist, and women's fiction, art, poetry, book reviews, feature-length pieces, and news. Offers MS guidelines (send for them with business-size envelope and 1 first-class stamp). Receives 500–700 fiction and poetry submissions per year. Receives 100–200 features submissions per year. Letter of query (with SASE) should precede MS submission. Responds to queries in 2–3 months. Responds to MSS submissions in 3–4 months. Accepts MSS not represented by agents. Accepts unsolicited MSS. Accepts MSS that are simultaneous submissions. Returns MSS with SASE. Feature MSS should be 15–20 pages, typed, double-spaced. Offers no payment. Tips: "We're really looking for balanced, well-written feature articles." Subscription information: 1 year—$9; 2 years—$17; Sample—$5. Anything in addition to these amounts is considered a tax-exempt donation.

IN STEP NEWSMAGAZINE

1661 North Water Street, Suite 411
Milwaukee, WI 53202
(414) 278-7840
E-mail: instepwi@aol.com
William Attewell

Publishes lesbian and gay nonfiction and news. Receives 24–50 MS and query submissions per year. Responds to queries in 2–3 weeks. Responds to MS submissions in 2–4 weeks. Accepts MSS not represented by agents. Accepts unsolicited MSS. Acceptance of MSS that are simultaneous submissions depends on geographic areas of distribution. Returns MSS with SASE. MSS should be no longer than 2–4 pages. MSS should be $8^1/_2$ x 11, typed, double-spaced. Dot-matrix submissions accepted (prefers letter quality). Pays on publication. Tips: "Brief, current, appeal to both gays and lesbians, in-season, submit time material 30 days prior to event/holiday." Subscription information: $35 per year (third class) $50 (first class)

IN THE FAMILY:
A MAGAZINE FOR LESBIANS, GAYS, BISEXUALS AND THEIR RELATIONS*

P.O. Box 5387
Takoma Park, MD 20913
(301) 270-4771
Fax: (301) 270-4660
E-mail: Lmarkowitz@aol.com

Publishes gay male and lesbian fiction, nonfiction, and essays. Offers MS guidelines (free on request). Receives 100 MS and query submissions per year. Responds to MS submissions in 4–6 weeks. Accepts MSS not represented by agents. Accepts unsolicited MSS. Does not accept MSS that are simultaneous submissions. MSS should be no more than 5,000 words. MSS should be typed, double-spaced, with author's name, address, phone, and e-mail (if appropriate) on first page.

IN TOUCH FOR MEN

13122 Saticoy Street
North Hollywood, CA 91605
(818) 764-2288
E-mail: alan@intouchformen.com
World Wide Web: http://www.intouchformen.com
Alan W. Mills

Publishes gay male erotic fiction, nude pictorials, humor, feature articles, and entertainment. Offers MS guidelines (send for them with business-size envelope and 1 first-class stamp). Receives 400–500 MS and query submissions per year. Responds to MS and query submissions in 1–2 months. MSS should be 2,500–3,500words. MSS should be typed, double-spaced. Prefers submissions on 3^1/$_2$-inch disks (Microsoft Word for Macintosh or saved in ASCII file format). Pays on publication; buys first North American serial rights. Sample issue available for $5.95. Tips: "Focus on the light-hearted, youthful, somewhat romantic side of erotic fiction. Don't be afraid to experiment. Safe-sex description in fiction a must."

ISLAND LIFESTYLE MAGAZINE

P.O. Box 11840
Honolulu, HI 96828
(808) 737-6400
Fax: (808) 735-8825
E-mail: ilm@tnight.com
World Wide Web: http://www.islandlifestyle.com
Cheryl L. Embry

Publishes lesbian and gay fiction, nonfiction, poetry, news, comics/cartoon strips, political, academic, and spirituality subjects. Receives 20 MS and query submissions per year. Accepts MSS not represented by agents. Accepts unsolicited MSS. Accepts MSS that are simultaneous submissions (writer should note in cover letter if MS has been submitted to other publications within the Hawaiian Islands). Prefers MSS to be 500–1,000 words.MSS should be 8^1/$_2$ x 11, typed, double-spaced. Dot-matrix submissions accepted. Prefers photos with features submissions. Include short bio. Pays on publication. Tips: "News features are best when they consist of nationally synthesized material of horizontal appeal. That is, they appeal to the greatest number of gays and lesbians and are national in scope."

THE JAMES WHITE REVIEW, A GAY MEN'S LITERARY QUARTERLY

P.O. Box 3356
Butler Quarter Station
Minneapolis, MN 55403
(612) 339-8317
Phil Willkie, Greg Hewett

Publishes gay male fiction, nonfiction, poetry, essays, and book reviews. Offers MS guidelines (send for them with business-size envelope and 1 first-class stamp). Receives 2,000 MS and query submissions per year. Responds to queries immediately. Responds to MS submissions in 3 months. Accepts MSS not represented by agents. Accepts unsolicited MSS. Does not accept MSS that are simultaneous submissions. Prose MSS should be no longer than 22 pages. Poetry MSS should be no longer than 10 pages. MSS should be typed, double-spaced, with page number and author's name on each page. Prefers submissions on disk. Letter-quality submissions and dot-matrix submissions accepted. Interested in submissions of art and photos (black and white only). Include short author's bio. Pays a small cash payment and 3 copies on publication. Tips: "We look at all submissions equally, without preference for better-known writers."Subscription information: 1 year—$14; 2 years—$24; Canada —$16; Foreign—$207; JWR Sustainer Club—$40 (tax deductible)

JOURNAL OF FEMINIST STUDIES IN RELIGION

Harvard Divinity School, Room 404
45 Francis Avenue
Cambridge, MA 02138
(617) 495-5751
Elizabeth Pritchard

Among other works, publishes lesbian nonfiction, poetry, political, and academic subjects. All work must deal with religious and feminist issues.

Offers MS guidelines (free on request). Receives 75–100 MS and query submissions per year. Responds to queries in 1 month. Responds to MS submissions in 3 months. Accepts MSS not represented by agents. Accepts unsolicited MSS. Does not accept MSS that are simultaneous submissions. MSS should be typed, double-spaced, with endnotes in the Chicago Manual of Style standard form. Submit 4 copies of MS. Offers no payment. Tips: "While we are an academic journal, we do see ourselves as rooted in and accountable to the feminist movement. One genre we publish is analytical reports of grassroots projects that might be taken up elsewhere."

JOURNAL OF GAY AND LESBIAN PSYCHOTHERAPY*

1439 Pineville Road
New Hope, PA 18938
David L. Scasta, MD

Publishes lesbian and gay nonfiction and academic subjects.

JOURNAL OF GAY AND LESBIAN SOCIAL SERVICES*

Department of Social Work
California State University, Long Beach
1250 Bellflower Boulevard
Long Beach, CA 90840-0902
James J. Kelly, PhD

Publishes lesbian and gay nonfiction and academic subjects.

JOURNAL OF HOMOSEXUALITY*

Center for Research & Education in Sexuality
San Francisco State University
Psychology Building, Room 502
San Francisco, CA 94132
John P. De Cecco, Ph.D.

Publishes lesbian and gay nonfiction and academic subjects.

JOURNAL OF LESBIAN STUDIES*

John Dewey Hall
Department of Psychology
University of Vermont
Burlington, VT 05405-0134
Esther D. Rothblum, Ph.D.

Publishes lesbian nonfiction and academic subjects.

KALLIOPE: A JOURNAL OF WOMEN'S ART

3939 Roosevelt Boulevard
Jacksonville, FL 32205
(904) 387-8211
Mary Sue Koeppel

Publishes fiction, poetry, and black-and-white art by women (no erotica). Reads MSS from September through April. Offers MS guidelines (free on request). Receives several thousand MS and query submissions per year. Responds to queries about interviews and reviews in 1 week. Responds to MS submissions in 3–6 months. Accepts MSS not represented by agents. Accepts unsolicited MSS. Does not accept MSS that are simultaneous submissions. Poetry MSS should not exceed 90 lines. Short fiction accepted. MSS should be letter quality. Black-and-white photo submissions accepted. Offers MS guidelines (free on request). Pays with 3 copies of publication. Tips: "We look for and publish excellence in poetry and fiction by women."

THE KENYON REVIEW

Kenyon College
Gambier, OH 43022
(614) 427-5208
Fax: (614) 427-5417
E-mail: kenyonreview@kenyon.edu
David Lynn

Publishes lesbian and gay fiction, poetry, essays, reviews, drama, and interviews. Offers MS guidelines (send for them with business-size envelope and 1 first-class stamp). Receives 3,600 MS and query submissions per year. Responds to MS submissions in 3 months. Accepts MSS not represented by agents. Accepts unsolicited MSS (read September 1 through March 31 only). Does not accept MSS that are simultaneous submissions. Does not accept electronic submissions. Fiction and nonfiction MSS should be no longer than 7,500 words. Poetry MSS should be no longer than 10 pages. MSS should be typed, double-spaced. Pays on publication.Tips: "The Kenyon Review is a general-interest, international quarterly journal of literature, culture, and the arts. While it takes pride in its leadership role in offering writers and readers opportunities to present and read works of great diversity in terms of gender, orientation, and form, its principal mission is the presentation of new works of outstanding literary and cultural importance and interest."

KICK PUBLISHING COMPANY*

Box 2222
Detroit, MI 48231
(313) 438-0704
Fax: (313) 963-4627
E-mail: kickpuco@aol.com
Curtis Lipscomb

Publishes lesbian and gay fiction, nonfiction, poetry, erotica, academic, religious, spirituality, historical, and news. Letter of query should precede MS submission. Responds to MS and query submissions in 2 weeks. Accepts MSS not represented by agents. Accepts unsolicited MSS. Accepts MSS that are simultaneous submissions. Does not return MSS. MSS should be typed, double-spaced. MSS should be 200–300 words. Prefers submissions on disk(PC). Pays on publication. Tips: "We love highly imaginative and highly informative information for and about African-American gays. We only publish the best work in our market."

KUMQUAT MERINGUE
P.O. Box 5144
Rockford, IL 61125
(815) 968-0713
E-mail: moodyriver@aol.com
Christian Nelson

Does not concentrate on lesbian and gay subjects but welcomes submissions from lesbian and gay writers. Publishes fiction and poetry. Offers MS guidelines (send for them with letter-size envelope and 1 first-class stamp). Responds to MS submissions in 6–8 weeks. Accepts MSS not represented by agents. Accepts unsolicited MSS. Accepts MSS that are simultaneous submissions. Returns MSS with SASE. MSS should be no longer than 500 words. Pays with 1 copy of publication. Subscription information: 3 issues—$8; Sample—$4

LAMBDA BOOK REPORT
P.O. Box 73910
Washington, DC 20056-3910
(202) 462-7924
Fax: (202) 462-5264
E-mail: LBREditor@aol.com
Jim Marks, Kanani Kauka

Publishes lesbian and gay book reviews and literary features. Letter of query should precede MS submission. Responds to queries in 3 weeks. Pays 30 days after publication. Tips: "Send a cover letter listing previous book reviewing experience, areas of interest, and expertise in reviewing, as well as 2–3 samples of published reviews." Subscription information: 6 issues—$19.95; 12 issues—$34.95

LAVENDER MAGAZINE*
2344 Nicollet Avenue South, Suite 130
Minneapolis, MN 55404
(612) 871-2237
Fax: (612) 871-2650
E-mail: SteveL.@lavender.scc.net

Publishes lesbian and gay poetry, news, historical, spirituality, and cultural subjects. Does not accept unsolicited MSS. Pays two weeks after publication.

LESBIAN CONNECTION
P.O. Box 811
E. Lansing, MI 48826
(517) 371-5257
Fax: (517) 371-5200
E-mail: elsiepub@aol.com
Sandy Taylor

Publishes lesbian news, letters, and articles from readers on any aspect of lesbian life (nonfiction). Accepts MSS not represented by agents. Accepts unsolicited MSS. Accepts MSS that are simultaneous submissions. MSS should be no longer than 2,500 words. MSS should be typed, double-spaced. Does not print poetry or fiction. The magazine is a lesbian free-style dialogue forum for lesbians across the country. Offers no payment.

THE LIBERTY PRESS*
P.O. Box 16315
Wichita, KS 67216-0315
(316) 262-8289
E-mail: librtyprs@aol.com
Vinnie Levin

Publishes lesbian and gay academic, religious, historical, spirituality, news, entertainment, current events. Receives 25 thousand query submissions per year. Responds to MS and query submissions in 1 month. Accepts MSS not represented by agents. Accepts unsolicited MSS. Accepts MSS that are simultaneous submissions.

LIBIDO: THE JOURNAL OF SEX & SENSIBILITY

P.O. Box 146721
Chicago, IL 60614
(773) 281-5839
Fax: (773) 275-0842
E-mail: rune@mcs.com
Jack Hafferkamp or Marianna Beck

Publishes gay, lesbian, male, and female fiction, nonfiction, poetry, and erotica. Offers MS guidelines (free on request with SASE). Receives over 500 MS and query submissions per year. Responds to MSS submissions within 6 months. Accepts MSS not represented by agents. Accepts unsolicited MSS. Accepts MSS that are simultaneous submissions (with indication that it is simultaneous). Returns MSS with SASE. Fiction and essay MSS should be no longer than 3,000 words. Review MSS should be no longer than 1,000 words. MSS should be typed, double-spaced. Macintosh computer disk (high density only) submissions accepted in Microsoft Word or MacWrite. Pays on publication. Tips: "We aim for excellence in writing; crisp wit and humor help a great deal." Subscription information: 4 issues—$30; Sample—$8

LOCK THE TARGET MEDIA/BACKSPACE*

25 Riverside Avenue
Gloucester, MA 01930-2552
(508) 283-2552
E-mail: charkim@tiak.net or
backspzine@aol.com
World Wide Web: http://www.tiac.net/users/ charkim
Kim Smith

Publishes lesbian and gay fiction, nonfiction, poetry, commentary, book reviews. Offers MSS guidelines (free on request; prefers SASE). Receives 120+ MS and query submissions per

year. Letter of query (with SASE) should precede MS submission. Responds to queries in 1 week. Responds to MS submissions in 2–4 weeks. Accepts MSS not represented by agents. Accepts unsolicited MSS. Accepts MSS that are simultaneous submissions. Returns MSS with SASE. MSS should be no more than 3,000 words for fiction, 500 words for poetry. MSS should be typed, double-spaced. Prefers letter-quality submissions. Pays with copy of publication.

LONG SHOT

P.O. Box 6238
Hoboken, NJ 07030
Danny Shot, Nancy Mercado, Lynne Breitfeller, Michael Kramer

Publishes lesbian and gay fiction, nonfiction, poetry, art, photographs. Responds to MS submissions in 12 weeks. Accepts MSS that are not represented by agents. Accepts unsolicited MSS. Accepts MSS that are simultaneous submissions. Returns MSS with SASE. MSS should be no longer than 12 pages. Pays with copies of publication. Subscription information: 2 years—$24

MALACHITE & AGATE*

6558 4th Section Road #149
Brockport, NY 14420
Marianne Milton

Publishes lesbian poetry, reviews, essays, letters, memoirs, and interviews. Offers MS guidelines. Letter of query should precede MS submission. Pays with copy of publication. Sponsors a poetry chapbook contest. Submit 20–25 pages of poetry and a $10 reading fee in the months of March or April. Include bio, acknowledgments, and SASE. Subscription information: 1 year—$7; 2 years—$12

MALEBOX MAGAZINE FOR BLACK GAY MEN*

P.O. Box 75392
Washington, DC 20013
(202) 543-5887
Fax: (202) 265-2608
E-mail: maleboxdc@aol.com

Publishes "the intimate opinions, experiences, and emotions of Black Gay Men." Publishes academic, fiction, nonfiction, poetry, historical, and spirituality subjects. Receives 100+ MS and query submissions per year. Responds to MS and query submissions in 1 month. Accepts MSS not represented by agents. Accepts unsolicited MSS. Accepts MSS that are simultaneous submissions. MSS should be no more than 5 typed, double-spaced pages. Tips: "Emotions, feelings, experiences are our forte."

MAMAROOTS *

P.O. Box 16151
Oakland, CA 94610-9991
(510) 238-9260
E-mail: mamaroots@aol.com
Asungi

Publishes lesbian academic, religious, historical, spirituality, news, and cultural subjects. Offers MS guidelines (send for them with business-size envelope and 1 first-class stamp). Tips: "We accept art and writing on Africa Goddess spirituality and African-womin-positive subjects."

MANIFEST READER

P.O. Box 14695
San Francisco, CA 94114
(415) 864-3456
Fax: (415) 863-7625
World Wide Web: http://www.manifestreader.com
John H. Embry

Publishes gay male leather and SM erotica. Offers MS guidelines. Prefers computer disk submissions. Responds to queries in 2 weeks. Responds to MS submissions in 30 days. Pays on publication. Tips: "Leather erotica with no legal ramifications."

MANSCAPE

P.O. Box 1314
Teaneck, NJ 07666
(201) 836-9177
Fax: (201) 836-5055
E-mail: firsthand3@aol.com
Bill Jaeger

Publishes gay male erotica. Receives 300 MS and query submissions per year. Responds to MS and query submissions in 4 weeks. Accepts MSS not represented by agents. Accepts unsolicited MSS. Does not accept MSS that are simultaneous submissions. Returns MSS with SASE. MSS should be typed, double-spaced. Pays 180 days after acceptance or on publication, whichever comes first. Tips: "Deal with reality; real people. Deal with genuine genitalia, not elephant trunks. Don't write about orgasms if you haven't experienced one. Truth is a turn-on." Subscription information: 1 year—$43.97

MENTOR*
P.O. Box 2917
Long Beach, CA 90801
(310) 495-1636
Kenneth O. Ulbrich

Publishes gay male erotica (older and younger).
Accepts MSS not represented by agents.
Accepts unsolicited MSS. Accepts MSS that are
simultaneous submissions. Returns MSS with
SASE. Pays on publication. Tips: "Sexual material about younger men (18+) who like being
with men they call 'Daddy' (any age)."

METRO SLAVE/SELECTIVE PUBLISHING, INC.*
P.O. Box 641610
Chicago, IL 60664-1610
(312) 332-7070
Fax: (312) 332-7170
E-mail: miley@metroslave.com
World Wide Web: http://www.metroslave.com
David A. Miley

Publishes gay male nonfiction, erotica, and
historical subjects. Letter of query (with SASE)
should precede MS submission. Responds to MS
submissions within 1 week. Accepts MSS not
represented by agents. Accepts unsolicited
MSS. Accepts MSS that are simultaneous submissions. Returns MSS with SASE. MSS should
be typed, double-spaced. Disk submission
accepted (ASCII, MSWord, PageMaker). Tips:
"Make it hot, make it violent. Make the characters young, fit, and smooth-skinned."

METROLINE
818 Farmington Avenue
Hartford, CT 06119
(860) 570-0823
Fax: (860) 570-1313
Michael G. Lauzier

Publishes lesbian and gay news, nonfiction,
features, and interviews. Offers MS guidelines
(send for them with business-size envelope
and 1 first-class stamp). Receives 50 query
submissions per year. Responds to query submissions in 3–5 weeks. Responds to MS submissions in 1–2 months. Accepts MSS not represented by agents. Accepts unsolicited MSS.
Accepts MSS that are simultaneous submissions. Returns MSS with SASE. MSS should be
no longer than 3,000 words. MSS should be
typed, double-spaced. Computer disk submissions accepted. Pays on publication. Tips: "Be
provocative."

MINNESOTA REVIEW
Department of English
East Carolina University
Greenville, NC 27858
(919) 328-6388
Jeffrey Williams

Concentrates on various issues in cultural politics, including lesbian and gay issues.
Publishes fiction, poetry, and academic subjects. Responds to queries in 2 weeks.
Responds to MS submissions in 2–4 months.
Accepts MSS not represented by agents.
Accepts unsolicited MSS. Returns MSS with
SASE. MSS should be typed, double-spaced.
Photocopied submissions accepted. Pays with
copies of publication. Subscription information: 1 year—$12; Institutions—$36/year

MODERN WORDS
350 Bay Street #100
Box 325
San Francisco, CA 94133
Garland Richard Kyle

Publishes lesbian and gay fiction, essays, poetry,
historical, and erotica. Responds to MS and
query submissions promptly. Accepts MSS not
represented by agents. Accepts unsolicited
MSS. Accepts MSS that are simultaneous submissions. Returns MSS with SASE. MSS should

be maximum of 10 pages for poetry and 20 pages for prose. MSS should be typed, double-spaced. Pays with two contributor's copies on publication.

THE NEW DAWN*

1761 G Street, N.W., Suite 6
Washington, DC 20009
(202) 667-1609

A correspondence club for gay women. Publishes relationship and friendship issues via correspondence.

THE NEW VOICE OF NEBRASKA

P.O. Box 3512
Omaha, NE 68103
Sharon Van Butsel

Publishes lesbian and gay nonfiction, poetry, news, political, historical, and religious subjects. Receives 150 MS and query submissions per year. Responds to MS and query submissions in 2-3 months. Accepts MSS not represented by agents. Accepts unsolicited MSS. Accepts MSS that are simultaneous submissions. Prefers submissions of 1,000 words or less. Offers no payment.

OBLIVION MAGAZINE*

519 Castro Street
San Francisco, CA 94114
(415) 487-5498
E-mail: oblivion@creative.net
World Wide Web: http://www.oblivionsf.com

Publishes gay and lesbian arts and entertainment.

OFF OUR BACKS

2337B 18th Street NW
Washington, DC 20009
(202) 234-8072
Fax: (202) 234-8092
E-mail: 73613.1256@compuserve.com

Publishes lesbian, women's, and feminist news, commentary, book and music reviews, and conference coverage. Does not publish poetry or fiction. Offers MS guidelines (free on request). Receives 400 MSS per year. Accepts unsolicited MSS. Query unnecessary, but include SASE and computer disk. Does not accept MSS that are simultaneous submissions. Responds to MS submissions in 3 months. MSS should be 6–12 pages, typed, double-spaced. Accepts photos, graphics, and art submissions. Pays with 1 copy of publication. Tips: "We are an international radical feminist newsjournal and are interested in writing by women about issues of interest to feminists (including international) with a feminist analysis."

OPEN HANDS

3801 N. Keeler Avenue
Chicago, IL 60641
(713) 736-5526
Fax: (713) 736-5475
Mary Jo Osterman

Publishes lesbian and gay religious and spirituality subjects. Offers MS guidelines (free on request). Receives 10 MS and query submissions per year. Letter of query should precede MS submissions. Accepts MSS not represented by agents. Accepts unsolicited MSS. Accepts MSS that are simultaneous submissions. Tips: "Each quarterly issue is on a theme. Interested writers should request listing of upcoming themes."

OPTIONS

P.O. Box 470
Port Chester, NY 10573
Diana Sheridan
E-mail: dianaeditor@aol.com

Publishes gay and bisexual male and lesbian/female erotic fiction and nonfiction. Offers MS guidelines (free on request). Responds to MS and query submissions in 3 weeks. Accepts MSS not represented by agents.

Accepts unsolicited MSS. Does not accept MSS that are simultaneous submissions. Returns MSS with SASE. MSS should be 2,000–3,000 words. MSS should be typed, double-spaced. Pays on publication. Tips: "Write hot. Make it safe sex or set it pre-AIDS." Subscription information: 1 year–19.90

THE ORANGE COUNTY BLADE
P.O. Box 1538
Laguna Beach, CA 92652
(714) 494-4898
Fax: (714) 376-9880
Bill La Pointe

Publishes lesbian and gay academic, erotica, news, and nonfiction. Offers MS guidelines (free on request). Letter of query should precede MS submission. Responds to MS and queries in 2 weeks. Accepts MSS not represented by agents. Accepts unsolicited MSS. Accepts MSS that are simultaneous submissions. Returns MSS with SASE. Pays on publication.

THE OTHER SIDE
300 W. Apsley Street
Philadelphia, PA 19144
(215) 849-2178
Mark Olson

A progressive Christian magazine for people seeking social justice and deeper spirituality. Publishes fiction, nonfiction, poetry, news, political, religious, spirituality, general social justice issues, and gay and lesbian issues. Offers MS guidelines (send for them with business-size envelope and 1 first-class stamp). Receives 600 MS and query submissions per year. Responds to queries in 1–2 weeks. Responds to MS submissions in 2–6 weeks. Send fiction MSS to Jennifer Wilkins, nonfiction MSS to Doug Davidson, and poetry MSS to Rod Jellema. Accepts MSS not represented by agents. Accepts unsolicited MSS.

Does not accept MSS that are simultaneous submissions. MSS should be no longer than 3,000 words. MSS should be typed, double-spaced. Dot-matrix submissions accepted. Pays 1 month after acceptance. Tips: "We are a Christian magazine with a commitment to peace, social justice, and human liberation. We have a strong interest in faith, art, and Christian spirituality. We have long included gay and lesbian Christians on our staff and among our readers. We have a vigorous commitment to gay and lesbian issues."

OUT MAGAZINE
110 Green Street, Suite 600
New York, NY 10012
(212) 334-9119
Sarah Pettit

Publishes lesbian and gay general interest material. Offers MS guidelines (free on request). Letter of query (with SASE) should precede MS submissions. Responds to MS and query submissions in 6 weeks. Accepts MSS not represented by agents. Accepts MSS that are simultaneous submissions. Returns MSS with SASE. MSS should be typed, double-spaced. Pays on publication; contract offered on longer pieces. Tips: "Advise writers to look at issue of magazine and obtain guidelines." Subscription information: 11 issues—$24.95 (basic rate)

OUT SMART MAGAZINE*
3406 Audubon Place
Houston, TX 77006
(713) 520-7237
Fax: (713) 522-3275
E-mail: outsmart1@aol.com
World Wide Web: http://www.outsmart-magazine.com
Greg Jou, Kyle Young

Publishes lesbian and gay nonfiction, religious, historical, spirituality, news, and health subjects.

Offers MS guidelines (send for them with 1 business-size envelope and 1 first-class stamp). Receives 90 MS and query submissions per year. Responds to queries in 1–2 months. Responds to MS submissions in 1 month. Accepts MSS not represented by agents. Accepts unsolicited MSS. Accepts MSS that are simultaneous submissions. MSS should be between 2,000–2,500 words. Pays on publication.

OWEN WISTER REVIEW
P.O. Box 3625
University Station
Laramie, WY 82071
(307) 766-6190
Editor

Publishes lesbian and gay fiction and poetry. Offers MS guidelines (send for them with business-size envelope and 1 first-class stamp). Receives 500 MS and query submissions per year. Responds to queries in 1–2 months. Reads MSS January through March and September through November. Accepts MSS not represented by agents. Accepts unsolicited MSS. Does not accept MSS that are simultaneous submissions. Returns MSS with SASE. MSS should be no longer than 14 pages. MSS should be typed, double-spaced. Photocopied submissions accepted. Pays with 1 copy of publication. Subscription information: 1 year—$10; Sample—$5

PERGAMON/WOMEN'S STUDIES INTERNATIONAL FORUM
Elsevier Science Ltd.
Langford Lane
Kislington OX5 1GB
United Kingdom
World Wide Web: http://www.elsevier.com/locate/wsif

A bimonthly journal to aid the distribution and exchange of feminist research in the multidis-

ciplinary, international area of women's studies and in feminist research. The policy of the journal is to establish a feminist forum for discussion and debate. Offers MS guidelines (free on request). Responds to MS submissions in 3 months. Accepts MSS not represented by agents. Accepts unsolicited MSS. Does not accept MSS that are simultaneous submissions. Returns MSS. Offers no payment.

PERIWINKLE*
Box 8052
Victoria, British Columbia V8W 3R7 Canada
(250) 382-5868
E-mail: hannah@islandnet.com
Tanya Yaremchuk

Publishes lesbian and gay fiction, erotica, poetry, and spirituality subjects. Offers MS guidelines (send for them with business-size envelope and 1 first-class stamp). Receives 150–200 MS and query submissions per year. Responds to queries in 1 month. Responds to MS submissions in 3–6 months. Accepts MSS not represented by agents. Accepts unsolicited MSS. Does not accept MSS that are simultaneous submissions. Returns MSS with SASE. MSS should be typed, double-spaced, numbered, with name on each page. Pays $5–$20.

PHOEBE
Women's Studies Department
State University of New York
Oneonta, NY 13820
(607) 436-2014
Fax: (607) 436-2656
Kathleen O'Mara

Publishes lesbian fiction, poetry, and academic subjects. Offers MS guidelines (free on request). Receives 500 MS and query submissions per year. Responds to queries in 30 days. Responds to MS submissions in 90 days. Accepts MSS not represented by agents.

Accepts unsolicited MSS. Accepts MSS that are simultaneous submissions. Returns MSS with SASE. MSS should be no longer than 30 pages. Submit MSS on 3$^1/_2$-inch disk (WordPerfect for Windows) along with 2 paper copies. MSS should be typed, double-spaced. Offers no payment.

PLEDGES & PADDLES*
P.O. Box 2048
231 W. 29th Street, Suite 905
New York, NY 10116-2048
(212) 736-6896
Fax: (212) 736-0255
E-mail: bobbg@aol.com
Lee Channower

Publishes gay male erotica. Offers MS guidelines (send for them with SASE). Responds to queries in 3 weeks. Reponds to MS submissions in 3 months. Accepts MSS not represented by agents. Accepts unsolicited MSS. Does not accept MSS that are simultaneous submissions. Returns MSS with SASE. Offers no payment. Tips: "Interests directed toward first-person experiences in male bondage and SM."

POETIC SPACE
P.O. Box 11157
Eugene, OR 97440
Don Hildenbrand

Publishes lesbian and gay fiction, nonfiction, poetry, and erotica. Offers MS guidelines (send for them with business-size envelope and 1 first-class stamp). Responds to MS and query submissions in 1–2 months. Accepts MSS not represented by agents. Accepts unsolicited MSS. Does not accept MSS that are simultaneous submissions. Returns MSS with SASE. MSS should be no longer than 2,000 words. Pays with copy of publication. Subscription information: 1 year—$10; 2 years—$18

POETRY MOTEL
1911 E. 1st Street
Duluth, MN 55812
Linda Erickson and Ed Gooder

Publishes lesbian and gay poetry. Offers MS guidelines (send for them with business-size envelope and 1 first-class stamp). Receives 1,000 MS and query submissions per year. Responds to queries in 1 week. Responds to MS submissions in 1 week to never. Accepts MSS not represented by agents. Accepts unsolicited MSS. Accepts MSS that are simultaneous submissions. Returns MSS with SASE. Prefers poetry MSS that are no longer than 1 page. Payment varies. Tips: "Sample *Poetry Motel* first to see what we are into. Send $6.95 and we'll send you something you've never seen before."

POSITIVELY AWARE
1258 W. Belmont
Chicago, IL 60657
(773) 404-8726
Fax: (773) 472-7505
E-mail: tpanet@aol.com
Brett Grodeck

Publishes HIV/AIDS news and nonfiction, health issues. Responds to MS and queries in 2–4 weeks. Accepts MSS not represented by agents. Accepts unsolicited MSS. Does not accept MSS that are simultaneous submissions. MSS should be no longer than 1,500 words. Pays on publication. Tips: "We are oriented primarily to HIV treatment issues. We discourage unsolicited personal stories and testimonials."

PRIMAVERA
Box 37-7547
Chicago, IL 60637

Publishes an annual of fiction and poetry that reflects the experiences of women of different ages, races, sexual orientations, social classes, and locations. Offers MS guidelines (send for them with business-size envelope and 1 first-class stamp). Responds to queries in 1–2 weeks. Responds to MS submissions in 2 weeks to 2 months. Accepts MSS not represented by agents. Accepts unsolicited MSS. Does not accept MSS that are simultaneous submissions. Returns MSS with SASE. Fiction MSS should be no longer than 6,000 words. MSS should be typed, double-spaced (single-spaced for poetry). Pays with 2 copies of publication.

QVOICE MAGAZINE*
P.O. Box 92385
Milwaukee, WI 53202
(414) 278-7524
Fax: (414) 272-7438
E-mail: qvoice@aol.com
World Wide Web: http://www.qvoice.com
William Attelwell

Publishes lesbian and gay lifestyle features, arts interviews, celebrity interviews, and occasional fiction. Receives 23–60 query MS submissions per year. Responds to MS and query submissions in 4–6 weeks. Accepts MSS not represented by agents. Accepts unsolicited MSS. Acceptance of MSS that are simultaneous submissions depends upon geographic areas of distribution. Returns MSS with SASE. MSS should be 1,500–2,000 words. MSS should be typed, double-spaced on $8^1/_2$ x 11-inch paper. Dot-matrix submissions not accepted. Accepts disk submissions (Mac or PC) if accompanied by hard copy. Pays on publication. "Tips: *Qvoice* is hip with a fresh attitude. Especially interested in interviews, the arts, humor, and culture." Subscription information: $50—1 year

QUEST
430 S. Broadway
Denver, CO 80209
(303) 722-5965
Fax: (303)698-1183
E-mail: questh@aol.com
Alex M. Paozols

Publishes lesbian and gay news, political, opinion, and general interest community coverage. Receives 30 MS and query submissions per year. Generally publishes only local writers.

RFD
P.O. Box 68
Liberty, TN 37095
(615) 536-5176
Short Mountain Collective

Publishes gay male fiction, nonfiction, poetry, erotica, news, political, academic, historical, religious, and spirituality subjects. Offers MS guidelines (free on request). Receives 100 MS and query submissions per year. Responds to MS and query submissions in 1 year. Accepts MSS not represented by agents. Accepts unsolicited MSS. Accepts MSS that are simultaneous submissions. Pays with 1 free copy of publication.

ROOM OF ONE'S OWN
P.O. Box 46160, Station D
Vancouver, BC, Canada V6J 5G5
(604) 871-0358
E-mail: wputman@direct.ca
Wendy Putman

Feminist literary journal by, for, and about women. Publishes fiction, poetry, creative nonfiction, essays, and reviews of recently released women's literature. Guidelines free on request. Receives 1,200 MS submissions per year. Publishes approximately 100 of received MSS. Responds to queries in 1–2 months. Responds to MS submissions in 6 months. Accepts MSS not represented by agents.

Accepts unsolicited MSS. Send SASE, with IRC when outside Canada. Does not return MSS. Send poems in groups of 4–5 poems, to 70 lines each, or single pieces of fiction, creative non-fiction, and essays, to 3,000 words. Pays small honorarium on publication, plus two copies of issue and a one-year subscription. Subscription information: 1 year—$32, 2 years—$50, Institutions—$38, back/sample issues—$7.

SAN FRANCISCO FRONTIERS MAGAZINE*
2370 Market Street, 2nd Floor
San Francisco, CA 94114
(415) 487-6000
Phil Julian

Publishes lesbian and gay academic, fiction, nonfiction, historical, spirituality, lifestyles, politics, entertainment, and news. Responds to MS and query submissions in 30 days. MSS should be no more than 2,000 words. Prefers disk submissions (PC-based word processing programs or text-only files). Pays on publication.

SBC MAGAZINE*
1155 4th Avenue
Los Angeles, CA 90019
(213) 733-5661
Fax: (213) 733-9200
E-mail: sbc@netwkcal.com
World Wide Web: http://www.sbc-online.com

Publishes black gay and lesbian academic, fiction, nonfiction, and news. Accepts MSS not represented by agents. Accepts unsolicited MSS. Returns MSS with SASE. Pays within 30 days of publication. Tips: "High-quality fiction, feature articles, and interviews from an Afrocentric homosexual viewpoint only."

SCOOP MAGAZINE*
2205 Wilton Drive
Fort Lauderdale, FL 33305-2131
(954) 561-9707
Brad Casey

Publishes gay male nonfiction, erotica, and news. Letter of query should precede MS submission. Reponds to queries in 2 weeks. Accepts MSS not represented by agents. Accepts unsolicited MSS. MSS should be typed, double-spaced. Pays per insertion.

SENSATIONS MAGAZINE
2 Radio Avenue #A5
Secaucus, NJ 07094
David Messineo

Publishes lesbian and gay fiction, poetry, and historical subjects. Offers MS guidelines (send for them with business-size envelope and 1 first-class stamp). Receives more than 200 MS and query submissions per year. Accepts MSS not represented by agents. Accepts unsolicited MSS. Accepts MSS that are simultaneous submissions. Returns MSS with SASE. Fiction MSS should be 5–35 pages. Poetry MSS should be no longer than 80 lines. MSS should be typed, double-spaced. Among the top 15 paying poetry markets in the U.S. since 1994. Offers up to $125 per poem, $75 per story on acceptance.

SING HEAVENLY MUSE!
P.O. Box 13320
Minneapolis, MN 55414
(612) 729-4266
Sue Ann Martinson

Publishes lesbian and women's fiction, nonfiction, and poetry. Offers MS guidelines (send for them with business-size envelope and 1 first-class stamp). Receives 2,000–3,000 MS and query submissions per year. Publishes 1 issue per year. Accepts MSS not represented by agents. Accepts unsolicited MSS. Prefers not to accept MSS that are simultaneous submissions. Returns MSS with SASE. Fiction and nonfiction MSS should be no longer than 6,000 words. Themes and reading periods are published in advance and can be sent for with SASE. Pays on publication. Subscription information: Individuals: 2 issues—$15 ; 3 issues—$20; 6 issues–$38; Institutions: 3 issues–$21; 6 issues–$40; Low income: 3 issues–$16; Sample–$4; Current issue–$8, plus $2 postage/handling.

THE SLANT: THE GAY, LESBIAN & BISEXUAL COMMUNITY OF MARIN
P.O. Box 629
Corte Madera, CA 94925
(415) 924-6635
Ed Wright

Publishes lesbian, gay, and bisexual news. Receives 1,000 MS and query submissions per year. Responds to MS and query submissions in 30 days. Accepts MSS not represented by agents. Accepts unsolicited MSS. Accepts MSS that are simultaneous submissions. Returns MSS with SASE. MSS should be 3–5 pages. MSS should be typed, double-spaced.

SNAKE NATION REVIEW
110 #2 West Force
Valdosta, GA 31601
(912) 249-8334
Nancy Phillips

Publishes lesbian and gay fiction, poetry, erotica, and spirituality subjects. Offers MS guidelines (send for them with business-size envelope and 1 first-class stamp). Receives 1,000 MS and query submissions per year. Responds to MS submissions in 3 months. Accepts MSS not represented by agents. Accepts unsolicited MSS. Accepts MSS that are simultaneous submissions. Returns MSS with SASE. Fiction and

essay MSS should be no longer than 5,000 words. Poetry MSS should be no longer than 100 lines. MSS should be typed, double-spaced. Dot-matrix submissions accepted. Pays on publication ($25 for stories and essays or prizes if in contest issue). Also publishes 1 collection of short stories and 1 poetry collection per year. Tips: "Literary, sophisticated."

SOJOURNER: THE WOMEN'S FORUM
42 Seaverns Avenue
Boston, MA 02130
(617) 524-0415
E-mail: sojourn@tiac.net
World Wide Web: http://www.tiac.net/users/sojourn/
Karen Kahn

Publishes women's fiction, nonfiction, poetry, news, and reviews from a feminist perspective. Offers MS guidelines (send for them with business-size envelope and 1 first-class stamp). Responds to queries in 4–6 weeks. Responds to MS submissions in 6–8 weeks. Accepts MSS not represented by agents. Accepts unsolicited MSS. Does not accept MSS that are simultaneous submissions. Returns MSS with SASE. MSS should be typed, double-spaced. Include biography. Pays $15 on publication, plus subscription. Subscription information: 1 year—$19; Sample—$3

SPECTATOR MAGAZINE
P.O. Box 1984
Berkeley, CA 94701
(510) 849-1615
E-mail: bold1000@aol.com or sexy@spectator-mag.com
Kat Sunlove

Publishes lesbian, gay, and straight nonfiction, news, academic, historical, and political subjects. Responds to MS and query submissions in 1–2 months. Accepts MSS not represented by agents. Does not accept unsolicited MSS. Accepts MSS that are simultaneous submissions. Returns MSS with SASE. Pays on publication.

SPSM&H MAGAZINE
329 E Street
Bakersfield, CA 93304
(805) 323-4064
Frederick A. Raborg, Jr.

Publishes lesbian and gay fiction, poetry, and erotica (romance or gothic fiction; sonnets or sonnet sequences for poetry). Offers MS guidelines (send for them with business-size envelope and 1 first-class stamp). Receives more than 1,000 MSS and query submissions per year. Responds to queries in 2 weeks. Responds to MS submissions in 2 weeks to 2 months. Accepts MSS not represented by agents. Accepts unsolicited MSS. Accepts MSS that are simultaneous submissions. Returns MSS with SASE. Fiction MSS should be no longer than 2,500 words. Pays on publication. Tips: "This is an opportunity for gay writers to express the romantic side of their relationships. We also use excellent drawings, related cartoons, and illustrations. Especially need nude male studies."

TACOMA'S OWN *
5601 N. 37th Street #QQ-4
Tacoma, WA 98407
(206) 756-0520
Ed Goldberg

Publishes lesbian and gay fiction, nonfiction, poetry, erotica, news, political, historical, and religious subjects. Accepts MSS not represented by agents. Accepts unsolicited MSS. Accepts MSS that are simultaneous submissions. Returns MSS with SASE. Offers no payment.

THIS WEEK IN TEXAS
811 Westheimer, Suite 111
Houston, TX 77006
(713) 527-9111
Fax: (713)527-8948
Alan Gellman

Publishes lesbian and gay news of Texas, political, events/photos, historical, fiction, and nonfiction. Offers MS guidelines (free on request). Receives 525 MS and query submissions per year. Responds to MS and query submissions in 1 month. Accepts MSS not represented by agents. Accepts unsolicited MSS. Accepts MSS that are simultaneous submissions. Returns MSS with SASE. MSS should be no longer than $2^1/_2$ pages, typed, double-spaced. Pays on publication.

TIKKUN MAGAZINE, A BIMONTHLY JEWISH CRITIQUE OF POLITICS, CULTURE, AND SOCIETY
26 Fell Street
San Francisco, CA 94102
(415) 575-1200

Publishes news, academic, historical, and religious subjects. Responds to queries in 2–3 weeks. Responds to MS submissions in 4 months. Accepts MSS not represented by agents. Accepts unsolicited MSS. Does not accept MSS that are simultaneous submissions. Returns MSS with SASE. MSS should be typed, double-spaced. Pays with free copies of publication. Tips: "Become familiar with the kinds of articles Tikkun prints by becoming a subscriber and regular reader."

TOUGH CUSTOMERS *
P.O. Box 410390
San Francisco, CA 94141-0390
(415) 252-1195
Fax: (415) 252-9574
Wickie Stamps

Publishes gay male erotica. Offers MS guidelines (send for them with business-size envelope and 1 first-class stamp). Receives 600 MS and query submissions per year. Responds to queries in 4–6 weeks. Accepts MSS not represented by agents. Does not accept unsolicited MSS. Accepts MSS that are simultaneous submissions. Returns MSS with SASE. MSS should be 1,500–5,000 words. MSS should be typed, double-spaced. Submit hard copy and disk. Pays 30 days after publication.

TRANSSEXUAL NEWS TELEGRAPH*
41 Sutter Street #1124
San Francisco, CA 94109
(415) 703-7161
E-mail: gailtnt@sirius.com, gailtnt@aol.com
Gail Sondegaard

Publishes transsexual and transgendered nonfiction, erotica, poetry, spirituality, and news subjects. Responds to queries in 1 month. Accepts MSS not represented by agents. Accepts unsolicited MSS. Accepts MSS that are simultaneous submissions. Returns MSS (with SASE). MSS should be typed, double-spaced. Tips: "Write well on transsexual/transgendered topics. Write about topics other than surgery."

TV/TS CHRONICLE*
855 E. Twain #123-547
Las Vegas, NV 89109
(561) 464-5447
Herman Nietzche

Publishes transgender erotica. Offers MS guidelines (send for them with business-size envelope and 1 first-class stamp).

VIEW MAGAZINE (A CHRONICLE OF GAY AND LESBIAN LIFE)*
P.O. Box 11067
Eugene, OR 97440
(514) 302-6523
E-mail: queergrl@darkwing.uoregon.edu
Kellee Weinhold, Kate Conley

Publishes lesbian and gay nonfiction, news, and cultural subjects. Offers MS guidelines (free on request). Receives 25–50 MS and query submissions per year. Responds to MS and query submissions in 2–4 weeks. Accepts MSS not represented by agents. Accepts unsolicited MSS. Accepts MSS not that are simultaneous submissions. Pays on publication. Tips: "Before submitting a manuscript, discuss your article idea with the editor to determine if a similar project is already in the works. The editor can provide guidance to help you focus your article. Because readers are best served by straightforward, objective information, manuscripts that appear biased or promotional will be rejected."

WHITE CRANE JOURNAL
P.O. Box 684704
Austin, TX 78768-4704
E-mail: tobyjohnso@aol.com
Toby Johnson

Quarterly journal exploring issues of gay male spirituality. Publishes gay male nonfiction, historical, and spirituality subjects. Offers MS guidelines (send for them with business-size envelope and 1 first-class stamp). Receives 25–30 MS and query submissions per year. Letter of query for longer works should precede MS submission. Responds to MS and query submissions in 2–3 weeks. Accepts MSS not represented by agents. Accepts unsolicited MSS. Accepts MSS that are simultaneous submissions. Returns MSS with SASE. MSS should be no more than

3,000 words. MSS should be typed, double-spaced. Letter-quality submissions preferred. Pays with 1 copy of publication. Tips: "Write with the assumption that the reader does not share your spiritual background. It is important to contextualize your religious language." Subscription information: 4 issues—$16

WHOREZINE
2300 Market Street #19
San Francisco, CA 94114
Vic St. Blaise

Publishes lesbian and gay nonfiction, erotica, news, academic, historical, religious, spirituality, travel, and art reviews. Responds to queries in 3–4 weeks. Responds to MS submissions in 4 weeks. Accepts MSS not represented by agents. Accepts unsolicited MSS. Accepts MSS that are simultaneous submissions. Returns MSS with SASE. MSS should be no longer than 1–2 pages. Tips: "We only accept work from current sex workers, former sex workers, and clients."

WOMEN & PERFORMANCE: A JOURNAL OF FEMINIST THEORY*
721 Broadway, 6th Floor, Performance Studies Department
New York, NY 10003
(212) 998-1652
Fax: (212) 995-4571
E-mail: jqj5170@is.nyu.edu
Judith Jerome

Publishes lesbian fiction, poetry, academic, dramatic writing, and interviews. Offers MS guidelines (send for them with business-size envelope and 1 first-class stamp). Receives 40 MS and query submissions per year. Responds to queries in 2 months. Responds to MS submissions in 3 months. Accepts MSS not represented by agents. Accepts unsolicited MSS. Accepts MSS that are simultaneous submissions.

Returns MSS with SASE. Pays with copies of publication. Tips: "Each issue is topic specific. Please query first. While we use some fiction, poetry, plays, we are primarily an academic journal."

WOMEN ARTISTS NEWS BOOK REVIEW
300 Riverside Drive
New York, NY 10025
(212) 666-6990
Cynthia Navaretta

Publishes book reviews and essays on art subjects, women artists, and women's issues. Offers MS guidelines (free on request). Receives 12–20 MS and query submissions per year. Letter of query should precede MS submission. Responds to queries in 2 months. Responds to MS submissions in 2 months. Accepts MSS not represented by agents. Accepts unsolicited MSS. Does not accept MSS that are simultaneous submissions. Returns MSS with SASE. MSS should be typed, double-spaced. Dot-matrix submissions accepted. Photo submissions accepted. Offers small payment. Subscription information: Individuals: 1 year—$1; Institutions: 1 year-$6

WOMEN IN THE LIFE MAGAZINE*
1436 U Street, NW, Suite 200
Washington, DC 20009
(202) 483-9818
Fax: (202) 483-4970
E-mail: witl@usbol.com
Sheila Alexander-Reid

Publishes lesbian fiction, nonfiction, poetry, and news.

ZERO HOUR

P.O. Box 766
Seattle, WA 98111
Jim Jones
(206) 286-2324

Publishes lesbian and gay fiction. Letter of
query (with SASE) should precede MS submission. Receives 200 MS and query submissions
per year. Responds to MS and query submissions in 2 months. Accepts MSS not represented
by agents. Accepts unsolicited MSS. Accepts
MSS that are simultaneous submissions.
Returns MSS with SASE. Pays $25 per short
story used. Also publishes 1 book per year.

Newspapers & Newsletters

AU COURANT NEWSMAGAZINE

P.O. Box 42741
Philadelphia, PA 19101-2741
(215) 790-1179
E-mail: pridewk@pond.com
World Wide Web: http://www.pond.com/~pridewk
Scott Mallinger

Publishes lesbian and gay nonfiction, news, and political subjects. Receives 300–350 MS and query submissions per year. Letter of query should precede MS submission. Accepts unsolicited MSS. Does not accept MSS that are simultaneous submissions. MSS should be 1,200–3,500 words. Pays on publication.

BAY AREA REPORTER

395 9th Street
San Francisco, CA 94103-3831
(415) 861-5019

Publishes lesbian and gay news, political and general entertainment features. Query letter should precede MS submission. Responds to query submission in 10 days. Send news queries to the attention of Mike Salinas. Send arts queries to Chris Culwell. Will return MSS if requested (with SASE). MSS should be 8$^{1}/_{2}$ x 11, typed, double-spaced. Writer can phone to discuss electronic transmittal. Pays on publication. Tips: "Don't make articles too long. Newspaper readers don't like lengthy discourses."

BLUE NIGHTS

P.O. Box 221841
Charlotte, NC 28222
(704) 531-9988
Fax: (704) 531-1361
E-mail: pridtype@vnet.net
Jim Yarbrough

Publishes gay male fiction and reviews; soft-core erotic short stories and gay male video reviews. Letter of query (with SASE) should precede MS submission. Responds to query submission in 2–4 weeks. Responds to MS submissions in 4–6 weeks. Accepts MSS not represented by agents. Accepts unsolicited MSS. Accepts MSS that are simultaneous submissions. Returns MSS with SASE. Fiction MSS should be 1,250–1,500 words. Review MSS should be 350–500 words. Pays on publication. Tips: "*Blue Nights* is distributed in gay clubs and adult bookstores free of charge. Therefore, our fiction must be soft-core due to our ease of availability. Stories must be more erotic than graphic."

BLUE RIDGE LAMBDA PRESS

P.O. Box 237
Roanoke, VA 24002
(540) 890-3184
Tom Winn

Publishes lesbian and gay nonfiction, news, and political subjects. Newsletter for the Roanoke Valley Gay and Lesbian Alliance.

COMMUNITY CONNECTIONS, INC.*

107 Cumberland Avenue #D
Asherville, NC 28801
(704) 251-2449
Fax: (704) 285-9390
Lisa Morpheu

Publishes gay, lesbian, bisexual, and transgender news and arts. Offers MS guidelines (free on request). Letter of query (with SASE) should precede MS submission. Responds to MS and query submissions in 1 month. Accepts MSS not represented by agents. Accepts unsolicited MSS. Accepts MSS that are simultaneous submissions. Returns MSS with SASE. Pays on publication. Tips: "Make sure your manuscript is neat and clean."

COMMUNITY NEWS

P.O. Box 663
Salem, OR 97308-0663
(503) 363-0006
Fax: (503) 363-0006
Chuck Simpson

Publishes lesbian and gay news, political, and religious subjects. Receives 20 MS and query submissions per year. Letter of query should precede MS submission. Responds to MS and query submissions in 2 days. Accepts unsolicited MSS.

DIVERSITY

P.O. Box 323
Boise, ID 84706
(208) 323-0805
E-mail: DiversityN@aol.com
World Wide Web: http://diversity.home.ml.org
Rich Keefe

Publishes lesbian and gay nonfiction, news, political subjects, and features. Receives 30–40 MS and query submissions per year. Responds to queries in 15–30 days. Accepts MSS not represented by agents. Accepts unsolicited MSS.

Computer disk submissions preferred. Offers no payment. Subscription information: 1 year—$15

THE DYKE RAG*

1122 E. Pike #1295
Seattle, WA 98122
(206) 720-4563
E-mail: kaytee0001@aol.com
Kate Tossey

Publishes lesbian news and variety. Pays on publication.

EIDOS

P.O. Box 96
Boston, MA 02137-0096
(617) 262-0096
E-mail: eidos@eidos.org
Brenda Loew

This is a publication of sexual freedom and erotic entertainment for women, men, and couples. Publishes fiction, nonfiction, poetry, news, erotica, political, historical, religious ("secular humanism"), and spirituality subjects. Offers MS guidelines (send for them with business-size envelope and 32¢ postage). Responds to MS and query submissions in 4–6 weeks. Accepts MSS not represented by agents. Accepts unsolicited MSS. Does not accept MSS that are simultaneous submissions. Returns MSS with SASE. MSS should be no longer than 1,500 words. MSS should be typed, double-spaced. Letter-quality submissions preferred. Pays with copy of publication. Tips: "We look for cutting-edge, avant-garde, progressive, provocative erotica depicting respectful, consensual images (in words and pictures) of the human form—sensual, sexual, explicit—as a liberating experience for all traditionally persecuted and oppressed sexual minorities." Subscription information: 4 issues–$25; Sample—$7

FRONT PAGE

P.O. Box 27928
Raleigh, NC 27611
(919) 829-0181
Fax: (919) 829-0830
E-mail: frntpage@aol.com
Jim Baxter

Publishes gay and lesbian news-related material. Letter of query (with SASE) should precede MSS submission. Accepts unsolicited MSS. Accepts MSS that are simultaneous submissions. Returns MSS with SASE. MSS should be typed, double-spaced. Pays on publication. Tips: "A North Carolina angle is a plus."

THE GAY AIRLINE & TRAVEL CLUB NEWSLETTER*

P.O. Box 69A04
West Hollywood, CA 90069
(213) 650-5112
Louis Wendruck

Publishes gay male erotica and travel.

GAY COMMUNITY NEWS (HONOLULU)

P.O. Box 37083
Honolulu, HI 96837
(808) 532-9000
E-mail: HawaiiGay1@aol.com
William E. Woods

Publishes lesbian and gay nonfiction features; news and gay guides to Hawaii. Receives 40–50 MS and query submissions per year. Letter of query should precede MS submission. Responds to MS and query submissions in 1 day to 2 months. Accepts MSS not represented by agents. Accepts unsolicited MSS. Accepts MSS that are simultaneous submissions. MSS should be no longer than 500 words. MSS should be typed, double-spaced, letter-quality. Photo submissions accepted. Pays on publication.

GAY SCENE

Regiment Publications
P.O. Box 247, Grand Central Station
New York, NY 10163
Bruce King

Publishes gay male nonfiction, erotica, and news. Letter of query should precede MS submission. Accepts MSS not represented by agents.

THE GAYLY OKLAHOMAN

P.O. Box 60930
Oklahoma City, OK 73146
(405) 528-0800
E-mail: gaylyok@aol.com
World Wide Web: http://www.gayly.com
Jack A. Wozniak

Publishes lesbian and gay news. Receives over 100 MS and query submissions per year. Letter of query (with SASE) should precede MS submission. Responds to MS and query submissions in 2 weeks. Accepts MSS not represented by agents. Accepts unsolicited MSS. Accepts MSS that are simultaneous submissions. Returns MSS with SASE (upon request). Dot-matrix submissions accepted. Computer disk submissions accepted (Macintosh). Submission deadlines are the 1st and 15th days of the month. Payment depends on submission. Tips: "The Gayly Oklahoman is a general interest news publication primarily intended for gay and lesbian readership, and is the only gay publication in the state of Oklahoma." Subscription information: 12 issues–$25; 24 issues–$35

THE GAZETTE
P.O. Box 2650
Brandon, FL 33509-2650
(813) 689-7566
Fax: (813) 654-6995
E-mail: thegazette@aol.com
Rand Hall

Publishes lesbian and gay news. Responds to MS and query submissions in 1–4 weeks, depending on timeliness of subject matter. Accepts MSS not represented by agents. Accepts unsolicited MSS. Accepts MSS that are simultaneous submissions. Does not return MSS. MSS should be no longer than 1,000 words. Tips: "We will edit for clarity and accuracy. Please include photos. Include as many details as possible." Subscription information: 12 issues—$18

HOMOSEXUAL INFORMATION CENTER NEWSLETTER*
P.O. Box 8252
Universal City, CA 91618
115 Monroe Street
Bossier City, LA 71111-4539
(318) 742-4709

Publishes lesbian and gay book reviews and sexuality subjects. Offers no payment.

JUST OUT NEWSPAPER
P.O. Box 14400
Portland, OR 97293-0400
(503) 236-1252
Fax: (503) 236-1257
E-mail: JustOut2@aol.com
Renée LaChance

Publishes lesbian and gay news, political subjects; movie, book, and theater reviews; and profiles. Receives 200 MS and query submissions per year. Responds to MS and query submissions in 1–3 months. Accepts unsolicited MSS. Accepts MSS that are simultaneous submissions to publications outside of Oregon. MSS should be no longer than 5 pages. Prefers MS submission by e-mail. MSS should be typed, double-spaced. Pays within 4 weeks after publication. Tips: "Be concise and crisp."

KEEP HOPE ALIVE*
P.O. Box 27041
West Allis, WI 53227
(414) 548-4344
World Wide Web: http://www.execpc.com/~keep-hope/keephope.html

Publishes nutrition, immunology, and AIDS nonfiction, news, and health subjects. Offers MS guidelines (free on request). Letter of query (with SASE) should precede MS submission. Responds to MS and query submissions in 2 weeks. Accepts MSS not represented by agents. Accepts unsolicited MSS. Accepts MSS that are simultaneous submissions. Returns MSS. MSS should by no more than 3 pages, typed, double-spaced.

KENTUCKY/OHIO/INDIANA WORDS
501 Madison Avenue, Suite 307
Indianapolis, IN 46225
(317) 632-8840
(317) 632-8840
E-mail: indword@iquest.net
World Wide Web: http://www.indword.com
Ted Fleishaker

Publishes gay male news and gossip. Offers MS guidelines (free on request). Receives 20 MS and query submissions per year. Responds to MS and queries in 2–3 weeks. Accepts MSS not represented by agents. Accepts unsolicited MSS. Accepts MSS that are simultaneous submissions. Returns MSS with SASE. MSS should be typed, double-spaced. Pays on publication.

KWIR PUBLICATIONS, INC./GAY PEOPLE'S CHRONICLE

P.O. Box 5426
Cleveland, OH 44101
(216) 631-8446
Fax: (216) 631-1082
E-mail: ChronOhio@aol.com
Martha Pontoni

Biweekly newspaper covering news, arts, and opinion in Ohio and the nation. Publishes lesbian and gay nonfiction and news. Receives 300–500 MS and query submissions per year. Prefers e-mail submissions in ASCII text; no attached files. Accepts MSS not represented by agents. Accepts unsolicited MSS. Accepts MSS that are simultaneous submissions. Returns MSS with SASE. MSS should be no longer than 600 words. Inquire with editor regarding payment. Subscription information: $1/2$ year—$15; 1 year—$30

LABYRINTH

P.O. Box 58489
Philadelphia, PA 19102
(215) 546-6686
E-mail: ltpwn@aol.com

Publishes news and features of interest to women. Returns MSS with SASE. MSS should be no longer than 2,000 words. Tips: "*Labyrinth* mainly does local news, although we will occasionally print articles about national feminist or lesbian issues."

LAMBDA GLBT COMMUNITY SERVICES*

910 N. Mesa, P.O. Box 31321
El Paso, TX 79931-0321
(915) 562-4297
E-mail: lambdaelp@aol.com
Rob Knight

Publishes gay, lesbian, bisexual, transgender nonfiction, news, and community events. Prefers e-mail submissions. Pays on publication.

LAS VEGAS BUGLE

P.O. Box 14580
Las Vegas, NV 89114-4580
(702) 369-6260
Fax: (702) 369-9325
Rob Schlegel

Publishes lesbian and gay news stories relating to Nevada and Las Vegas.

LESBIAN AND GAY NEW YORK*

150 5th Avenue, Suite 600
New York, NY 10011
(212) 691-1100, ext. 20
Fax: (212) 691-6185
Troy Masters

Publishes lesbian and gay arts and entertainment, and news. Offers MS guidelines (send for them with business-size envelope and 1 first-class stamp). Receives 250 MS and query submissions per year. Responds to MS and query submissions in 3 weeks. Accepts MSS not represented by agents. Accepts unsolicited MSS. Accepts MSS that are simultaneous submissions outside the greater New York market. Returns MSS with SASE. Pays after publication. Tips: "We are most interested in issues of concern to New York readers and significant stories from outside New York that are specially suited to report."

LESBIAN HERSTORY ARCHIVES NEWSLETTER*

Lesbian Herstory Educational Foundation, Inc.
P.O. Box 1258
New York, NY 10116
(718) 768-3953
Fax: (718) 768-4663

Publishes all aspects of lesbian culture and the

work of the Lesbian Herstory Archives. Collects MSS for readers/researchers to use on site. Tips: "We hope lesbian writers will consider sending a copy of their manuscripts to the Archives for the historical record while they continue to pursue publication elsewhere. This way, published elsewhere or not, their original work will not be lost to history."

LESBIAN NEWS
P.O. Box 55
Torrance, CA 90508
(310) 656-2692
E-mail: theln@earthlink.net

Publishes news and features oriented to lesbians. Letter of query (with SASE and phone number) should precede MS submission. Accepts unsolicited MSS. Offers small payments for articles involving reporting. Tips: "Read the publication thoroughly to see if your material would be appropriate."

THE LESBIAN REVIEW OF BOOKS*
P.O. Box 6369
Altadena, CA 91003-6369
(818) 398-4200
Fax: (818) 398-4200
Loralee MacPike

Publishes reviews of lesbian/feminist books. All reviews are commissioned. Does not accept unsolicited reviews. Pays with copy of publication. Tips: "Send letter with areas in which you would like to review and your qualifications in those areas. We will respond."

MAMA BEARS NEWS & NOTES
6536 Telegraph
Oakland, CA 94609
(510) 428-9684
Fax: (510) 654-2774
Alice Molloy

Publishes book reviews on lesbian and women's fiction, nonfiction, poetry, psychology, erotica, health, news, political, academic, historical, religious, and spirituality subjects. Accepts unsolicited reviews. Does not accept reviews that have been published elsewhere. Returns MSS with SASE. Offers no payment.

MARQUISE*
P.O. Box 701204
San Antonio, TX 78232

Publishes lesbian and gay news. Offers MS guidelines (free on request). Receives 20–30 MS and query submissions per year. Responds to queries in 1 month. Responds to MS submissions in 3–6 months. Accepts MSS not represented by agents. Accepts unsolicited MSS. Accepts MSS that are simultaneous submissions. MSS should be less than 5,000 words. Prefers submission on disk (ASCII or TXT).

THE MILITARY & POLICE UNIFORM ASSOCIATION NEWSLETTER*
P.O. Box 69A04
West Hollywood, CA 90069
(213) 650-5112
Louis Wendruck

Publishes gay male erotica and uniform interest.

MISSISSIPPI VOICE*
P.O. Box 7737
Jackson, MS 39248-7737
Fax: (601) 354-2251
E-mail: missvoice@aol.com
Michael Breazeale

Publishes lesbian and gay news.

MOM GUESS WHAT NEWSPAPER

1725 L Street
Sacramento, CA 95814
(916) 441-NEWS
Linda Birner

Publishes lesbian and gay news, political, academic, historical, and entertainment subjects. Offers MS guidelines (send for them with business-size envelope and 1 first-class stamp). Receives over 50 article and query submissions per year. Letter of query (with SASE) should precede article submission. Responds to article and query submissions in 1 week. Accepts unsolicited articles. Accepts articles that are simultaneous submissions. Returns articles with SASE. Articles should be 3–7 double-spaced pages. Payment varies, but usually on publication.

MOM'S APPLE PIE

P.O. Box 21567
Seattle, WA 98111
(206) 325-2643

Publishes lesbian nonfiction, news, political subjects; children's art and writing. Material should be related to lesbian and gay parents and their children. Receives 3–4 MS and query submissions per year. Responds to queries in 4–6 weeks. Responds to MS submissions in 4–8 weeks. Accepts MSS not represented by agents. Accepts unsolicited MSS. Accepts MSS that are simultaneous submissions. Returns MSS with SASE. MSS should be no longer than 1,000 words. Pays with 3 copies of publication and 1 year subscription. Tips: "We appreciate personal experiences and insights, especially when they may be generalized to help others. Black-and white-graphic art and humor welcome." Subscription information: 1 year—$15

MOMAZONS

P.O. Box 82069
Columbus, OH 43202
(614) 267-0193
Kelly A. McCormick

Publishes writing by lesbian mothers and lesbian mothers-to-be on issues concerning lesbian families, lesbian parenting. Offers MS guidelines (send for them with business-size envelope and 1 first-class stamp). Receives more than 100 MS and query submissions per year. Responds to queries in 1–2 weeks. Responds to MS submissions in 2–4 weeks. Accepts MSS not represented by agents. Accepts unsolicited MSS. Accepts MSS that are simultaneous submissions. Returns MSS with SASE. Offers no payment. Subscription information: Sliding scale, $15–$25; Institutional/ organizational membership: $30

MOUNTAIN PRIDE MEDIA, INC./OUT IN THE MOUNTAINS

P.O. Box 177
Burlington, VT 05402
E-mail: oitm@together.net
World Wide Web: http://members.aol.com/oitm/
Hugh Coyle, Steven West

Publishes gay, lesbian, bisexual, and transgender news primarily of interest to Vermont and similarly rural areas. Receives 100 MS and query submissions per year. Responds to queries in 2 weeks to 1 month. Responds to MS submissions in 2–4 weeks. Accepts MSS not represented by agents. Accepts unsolicited MSS. Accepts MSS that are simultaneous submissions. Returns MSS with SASE. Offers no payment at present. Subscription information: 1 year—$20

ΑΑΑ

NORTH BI NORTHWEST/SEATTLE BISEXUAL WOMEN'S NETWORK*
P.O. Box 30645
Greenwood Station
Seattle, WA 98103-0645
(206) 517-7767
E-mail: sbwn@usa.net

Publishes bisexual and women's fiction, poetry, book and movie reviews.

OBSERVER
P.O. Box 50733
Tucson, AZ 85703
(520) 622-7176
Fax: (520) 792-8382
E-mail: watcher@azstarnet.com
World Wide Web: http://bonzo.com/observer
Bob Ellis

Publishes lesbian and gay news, political, academic, and religious subjects. Returns MSS with SASE.

OF A LIKE MIND
Box 6677
Madison, WI 53716
(608) 257-5858
Lynnie or Jade

International newspaper and network for, by, and about goddess women. Publishes spiritually positive and woman-centered subject matter. Offers MS guidelines (free on request). Letter of query should precede MS submission. MSS should be typed, double-spaced, or submitted on disk (Microsoft Word or text file). Pays with copies of publication.

OUR HORIZONS
P.O. Box 92396
Milwaukee, WI 53202-0396
(414) 445-5552
Ralph F. Navarro

Publishes gay news, political, religious, and spirituality subjects.

OUR OWN
739 Yarmouth Street
Norfolk, VA 23510
(757) 625-0700
Fax: (757)625-6024
Kirk Read

Publishes gay, lesbian, bisexual, and transgender nonfiction, news, political, historical, and events/activities in the state of Virginia. Accepts unsolicited MSS. Accepts MSS that are simultaneous submissions. Returns MSS with SASE. MSS should be 8½ x 11, typed, double-spaced. Letter-quality submissions preferred. Accepts e-mail submissions. Accompanying photography submissions accepted. Pays on publication. Subscription information: 1 year—$20

OUT
747 South Avenue
Pittsburgh, PA 15221
(412) 243-3350
Fax: (412) 243-7989
E-mail: pghsout@aol.com
Jeff Howells

Publishes lesbian and gay news, features, and entertainment. Receives 25–50 MS and query submissions per year. Responds to MS and query submissions in 3–4 weeks. Send MSS to David Doorley, Features Editor. Accepts MSS not represented by agents. Accepts unsolicited MSS. Accepts MSS that are simultaneous submissions. Returns MSS with SASE. MSS should be 750-1,200 words. MSS should be 8½ x 11, typed, double-spaced. Also sponsors an annual gay and lesbian fiction contest. Deadline is usually May 31. First prize is $100 and publication of story; 2,500 word limit; no explicit sex. Pays on publication. Tips: *"Out* is primarily interested in receiving national news stories and entertainment features."

OUTWORD NEWSMAGAZINE*
709 28th Street
Sacramento, CA 95816-4116
(916) 329-9280
Fax: (916) 498-8445
E-mail: outwordmag@aol.com
World Wide Web: http://www.vtpride.org
Erich Mathias

Publishes lesbian and gay news. Offers MS guidelines (send for them with SASE). Responds to MS and query submissions in 2–3 weeks. Accepts MSS not represented by agents. Accepts unsolicited MSS. Accepts MSS that are simultaneous submissions. MSS should be typed, double-spaced. Letter-quality preferred. MSS can be submitted on disk (ASCII text) or by e-mail. Pays on publication. Tips: "Submit news samples and features first. Ask for specific article/topic. Submit within specified deadline."

PHILADELPHIA GAY NEWS
505 S. Fourth Street
Philadelphia, PA 19147
(215) 625-8501
Fax: (215) 925-6437
E-mail: masco@aol.com
World Wide Web: http://epgn.com
Patti Tihey

Publishes lesbian and gay news, features, and opinion. Primary focus is local news, but accepts submissions about important issues and people nationwide. Write for guidelines. Pays on publication.

THE PINK PAPER
P.O. Box 6462
Syracuse, NY 13217-6462

Publishes lesbian and gay news and political subjects. Responds to queries in 4 weeks.

PRIDE ACCESS CORP.*
33523 Eight Mile Road #185A-3
Livonia, MI 48152
(810) 615-7003
Fax: (810) 615-7018
E-mail: pridepblis@aol.com
World Wide Web:
http://members.aol.com/BeThLines

Publishes gay and lesbian news. Accepts MSS not represented by agents. Accepts unsolicited MSS. Does not accept MSS that are simultaneous submissions. Pays by the word.

QMONTHLY*
10 S. 5th Street, Suite 200
Minneapolis, MN 55402
(612) 321-7300
(612) 321-7333
Rick Nelson

Publishes lesbian and gay features and news. Accepts unsolicited MSS. Accepts MSS that are simultaneous submissions if local exclusive. MSS should be no more than 2,500 words. Pays on publication.

Q-NOTES

P.O. Box 221841
Charlotte, NC 28222
(704) 531-9988
Fax: (704) 531-1361
E-mail: pridtype@vnet.net
World Wide Web: http://www.q-notes.com
Jim Yarbrough, David Stout

Q-Notes is a 10-year-old gay newspaper published every other week in Charlotte, N.C. It is distributed free throughout North and South Carolina in nightclubs, restaurants, mainstream and adult bookstores, and some retail outlets. Q-Notes is also available by subscription. Each issue of Q-Notes contains news, features, columns, personals, classifieds, and calendar information. Subscription information: 12 issues–$25 (bulk mail, $15) 25 issues–$52 (bulk mail, $28)

SEATTLE GAY NEWS

1605 12th Avenue, Suite 31
Seattle, WA 98122
(206) 324-4297
Fax: (206) 322-7188

Publishes lesbian and gay news, political, academic, historical, religious, spirituality, and articles of interest to the gay and lesbian community. Looking for humor submissions. Responds to MS and query submissions in 4 weeks. Accepts MSS not represented by agents. Accepts unsolicited MSS. Accepts MSS that are simultaneous submissions. MSS should be typed, double-spaced. Dot-matrix submissions accepted. Pays on publication. Tips: "Get to the point."

SECOND STONE

P.O. Box 8340
New Orleans, LA 70182
(504) 899-4014
E-mail: secstone@aol.com
James Bailey

Publishes lesbian and gay news and religious subjects. Receives 50 MS and query submissions per year. Letter of query (with SASE)

should precede MS submission. Responds to MS and query submissions in 4 weeks. Accepts MSS not represented by agents. Accepts unsolicited MSS. Accepts MSS that are simultaneous submissions. MSS should be no longer than 1,200 words. MSS should be typed, double-spaced. Computer disk submissions accepted (Macintosh, MacWrite, Microsoft Word). Dot-matrix submissions accepted. Pays on publication.

SOUTHERN VOICE

1095 Zonolite Road
Atlanta, GA 30306
E-mail: southvoice@aol.com

Publishes lesbian and gay news, arts, entertainment, and features. Offers MS guidelines (send for them with letter-size envelope and 1 first-class stamp). Receives several hundred MS and query submissions per year. Letter of query should precede MS submission. Accepts MSS not represented by agents. Accepts unsolicited MSS. Accepts MSS that are simultaneous submissions (except in Atlanta market). Does not return MSS. Prefers sumbissions by e-mail. MSS should be typed, double-spaced. Dot-matrix submissions accepted. Pays at end of month following publication. Tips: "Follow-up phone calls for queries or unsolicited MSS are strongly discouraged. Photo availability increases chance that story will be accepted. Query in writing only."

STONEWALL JOURNAL*

P.O. Box 10814
Columbus, OH 43101
(614) 299-7764
Fax: (614) 299-4408
E-mail: stnwall@ix.netcom.com,
jsolari@freenet.columbus.oh.us
World Wide Web: http://www.stonewall-columbus.org
Jan Solari

Publishes lesbian and gay news, reviews, and interviews. Pays on publication.

STONEWALL NEWS

P.O. Box 3994
Spokane, WA 99220-3994
(509) 456-8011
Fax: (509) 455-7013
Jon M. Deen

Publishes lesbian and gay news.

THIS MONTH IN MISSISSIPPI

P.O. Box 8342
Jackson, MS 39284-8342
(601) 372-7979
Eddie Sandifer

Publishes lesbian and gay fiction, nonfiction, poetry, news, political, academic, historical, and religious subjects. Responds to queries in 1 week. Tips: "We welcome short news items on the military, AIDS, child custody, divorce cases, court reports, gay-bashing, or anything about the right-wing elements in the world." Subscription information: 1 year—$15

TLB (THE LOVING BROTHERHOOD NEWSLETTER)*

P.O. Box 556
Sussex, NJ 07461
(201) 875-4710
Ralph H. Walker

Publishes gay male nonfiction, academic, poetry,

and spirituality subjects. Offers MS guidelines (send for them with SASE). Accepts MSS not represented by agents. Accepts unsolicited MSS. Does not accept MSS that are simultaneous submissions. Returns MSS with SASE. MSS should be no more than 1,000 words. Pays with subscriptions or memberships.

TREATMENT ISSUES*

129 W. 20th Street, 2nd Floor
New York, NY 10011
Fax: (212) 337-3656
E-mail: dave_g@gmhc.org
David Gilden

Publishes AIDS treatment news and health subjects. Receives 12 MS and query submissions per year. Responds to queries in 1 months. Responds to MS submissions in 2 months. Accepts MSS not represented by agents. Accepts unsolicited MSS. Does not accept MSS that are simultaneous submissions. Prefers submissions on disk. Pays on publication. Tips: "Clear writing is essential. Writers have to explain technical issues to a nontechnical audience."

TULSA FAMILY NEWS*

P.O. Box 4140
Tulsa, OK 74159
(918) 583-1248
Fax: (918) 583-4615
E-mail: tulsanews@aol.com
World Wide Web: http://users.aol.com/tulsanews/

Publishes lesbian, gay, bisexual, transgender news.

TWN (THE WEEKLY NEWS, INC.)

901 NE 79th Street
Miami, FL 33138
(305) 757-6333 x. 8910
Fax: (305) 756-6488
E-mail: news@twnmag.com
Doug Janousik

Publishes lesbian and gay nonfiction, news, academic, historical, and religious subjects. Offers MS guidelines. Receives over 100 MS and query submissions per year. Responds to queries in 2–3 weeks. Responds to MS submissions in 3–4 weeks. Accepts MSS not represented by agents. Accepts unsolicited MSS. Accepts MSS that are simultaneous submissions (except in South Florida market). Returns MSS with SASE. MSS should be typed, double-spaced. Dot-matrix submissions accepted. Pays on publication. Tips: "Keep our South Florida audience in mind. *TWN* competes in a market with 3 alternatives, but *TWN* is the gay only alternative. We thrive on breaking news and features with a South Florida angle." Sample copy—$2.

WINDY CITY TIMES SENTURY PUBLICATIONS

325 W. Huron, Suite 510
Chicago, IL 60610
(312) 397-0025
Fax: (312) 397-0021
E-mail: editor@wctimes.com
World Wide Web: http://www.wctimes.com
Jeff McCourt

Publishes lesbian and gay news, political, religious, entertainment, and personal views. Receives 50–100 MS and query submissions per year. Responds to MS and query submissions in 2–3 weeks. Accepts MSS not represented by agents. Accepts unsolicited MSS. MSS for features should be a minimum length of 1,200 words and a maximum length of 2,000 words. MSS should be $8^{1}/_{2}$ x 11, typed, double-spaced. Pays at the end of the month of publication.

WOMAN'S MONTHLY

1001 N. Highland Street
Arlington, VA 22201
(703) 527-4881
Fax: (703) 527-9342
E-mail: womopub@aol.com

A monthly calendar publishing lesbian and feminist-oriented nonfiction, how-to, health, and spirituality subjects. Offers MS guidelines (free on request). Receives 20–30 MS and query submissions per year. Letter of query (with SASE) must precede MS submission. Responds to queries in 1 month. Accepts MSS not represented by agents. Does not accept unsolicited MSS. Does not accept MSS that are simultaneous submissions. Returns MSS with SASE. All articles are short (approximately 600 words). Fiction, poetry, and erotica not published. MSS should be typed, double-spaced. Prefers electronic or disk submissions. Pays in copies of publication. Tips: "We're looking for good profiles of lesbians in the Washington, DC, area; nonfiction based on strong research or accessible personal experience; and sports-oriented pieces. We're eager to give emerging writers a chance, but they must be willing to have their work edited for style. We're always looking for new ideas for articles; women's health issues, young lesbians' issues, aging, violence, etc."

WOMYN'S PRESS

P.O. Box 562
Eugene, OR 97440
(541) 302-8146

A feminist newspaper with a large lesbian content. Publishes feminist fiction, nonfiction, poetry, news, political, historical, and spirituality subjects. Ongoing "Fat Womyn" features. Offers MS guidelines (send for them with 10 x

13 envelope and 3 first-class stamps).
Responds to MS and query submissions within
9 months. Accepts MSS not represented by
agents. Accepts unsolicited MSS. Accepts MSS
that are simultaneous submissions (but writer
should inform as to where else submissions are
sent). MSS should be typed, double-spaced,
but will consider any readable MS. Pays with
one-year subscription.

WOMYN'S WORDS
P.O. Box 15548
St. Petersburg, FL 33733-5548
(813) 823-5353

Publishes lesbian news and political subjects
and local activities. Subscription information:
1 year—$15, bulk rate; $20 first class

THE WORD*
(317) 632-8840
Fax: (317) 687-8840
E-mail: IndWord@iquest.net
World Wide Web: http://www.indword.com
Ted Fleishaker

Publishes lesbian and gay news.

THEATERS

CIRCA NOW PRESENTS
P.O. Box 14912
Portland, OR 97214
(503) 735-4444
Howie Baggadonutz

Produces "pre-packaged" shows (e.g., touring one-person works, musical revues, comedies). Submit introductory letter with reviews, demo tape, SASE postcard. Gay/lesbian themes preferred.

THE GLINES
240 West 44th Street
New York, NY 10036
John Glines

Accepts unsolicited scripts. Submit full script with synopsis and SASE. Occasionally produces musicals and one-acts. Considers scripts that have been previously produced (outside of New York). Script must have a gay theme. Prefers scripts with no more than 10 cast members. Responds to script submissions in 2 months. Pays per performance or royalties.

THE GROUP (THEATRE WORKSHOP)
436 Hawthorne #2
Houston, TX 77006
(713) 522-2204
Joe Watts

Accepts unsolicited scripts. Offers script guidelines (send for them with business-size envelope and 1 first-class stamp). Returns scripts with SASE. Submit synopsis, followed by full script on request. Produces 2-3 plays per year. Produces musicals and one-acts. Considers scripts that have been previously produced. Considers scripts that have been produced in workshop. Gay subject matter only. Does not produce under any Equity contracts. Pays royalties.

KALIYUGA ARTS
141 Albion Street
San Francisco, CA 94110
(415) 431-8423
John Sowle and Steven Patterson

Accepts unsolicited scripts. Returns scripts with SASE. Submit full script, typed. Has produced, and will consider, musicals and one-acts. Considers scripts that have been previously produced. Considers scripts that have been produced in workshop. Does not produce under any Equity contracts, but has produced, under the Bay Area Project Policy agreement which permits Equity members to participate in productions being presented in houses under 100 seats for a limited number of performances without a contract. Payment negotiated. Tips: "We're looking for plays that are complex, literate, and intelligent; plays as wild, messy, and ambiguous as the lives most of us lead. Polemics don't interest us. Flawed, human characters do. No fluff, please. We're a tiny two-man operation with no performance space of our own and produce only when we find material that really speaks to us and that we feel we absolutely have to do."

LAMBDA PLAYERS OF SACRAMENTO
919 20th Street
Sacramento, CA 95814
(916) 491-1062
E-mail: chaspeer@pacbell.net
Michael D. Jackson

In eigth year of operation. Produces musicals, one-acts, and full-length plays. Accepts unsolicited scripts. Returns scripts with SASE. Submit full script with synopsis and reviews (if available). Considers plays that have been previously produced. Considers plays that have been previously produced in workshop. Scripts should target gay, lesbian, bisexual, and transgender audiences or issues pertaining to them (i.e., discrimination, equality, etc.). Prefers 5–7 cast members, but will consider larger cast. Does not produce under any Equity contracts and operates as a nonprofit project of Sacramento's Lambda Community Center. Royalties determined per project. Performances are in a 49- or 300-seat theater, dependent on production requirements.

THE PURPLE CIRCUIT
2025 Griffith Park Boulevard #4
Los Angeles, CA 90039
(213) 661-1982
E-mail: purplecir@aol.com
Bill Kaiser

A networking organization promoting gay, lesbian, queer, bi, and transgender theater. Publishes in *The Purple Circuit,* a quarterly newsletter, the Purple Circuit Directory, which lists such theaters around the U.S. and abroad. Operates the Purple Circuit Hotline (213) 666-0693), which lists currently running gay and lesbian shows in California and elsewhere.

RED HEN PRODUCTIONS*
P.O. Box 91926
Cleveland, OH 44104-3926
(216) 631-4301
E-mail: redhennet@aol.com
Amanda T. Shaffer

Accepts unsolicited scripts. Produces lesbian plays, performance art, poetry readings, and dance. Offers script guidelines (free on request). Receives 125 script submissions per year. Letter of query (with SASE) should precede script submission. Responds to queries in 1 week to 1 month. Responds to script submissions in 6 months to 1 year. Scripts should be bound or in folder. Royalties paid on production.

SUN ERGOS: A COMPANY OF THEATER AND DANCE
2203-700 9th Street, S.W.
Calgary, Alberta, Canada T2P 2B5
(403) 264-4621
E-mail: waltermoke@sunergos.com
Robert Greenwood, Dana Luebke

Accepts unsolicited scripts. Returns scripts with SASE. Submit letter with synopsis. Full script requested if interested. Produces one-acts. Considers scripts that have been previously produced. Considers scripts that have been produced in workshop. Prefers short monologues, character studies, and short plays for 1 or 2 characters or for 2 people to play multiple roles. Scripts should emphasize the humanity of the situation or event. Produces as an Equity cooperative. Responds to script submissions in 3 months. Pays royalties.

SWEET CORN PRODUCTIONS

Box 9685
Seattle, WA 98109
(206) 935-1206
E-mail: demian@buddybuddy.com
World Wide Web: http://buddybuddy.com
Steve Bryant and Demian

Accepts unsolicited scripts. Submit letter and one-page synopsis. Scripts should be typed or computer-printed. Produces musicals and one-acts. Considers scripts that have been previously produced. Considers scripts that have been produced in workshop. Scripts should have small cast. Does not produce under any Equity contracts. Special consideration for stories supporting male couples and female couples. Tips: "Not accepting scripts at this time. We produce stage, video, and radio pieces on themes of liberation and hope. Always send SASE."

THEATER RHINOCEROS

2929 16th Street
San Francisco, CA 94103
(415) 552-4100
Fax: (415) 558-9044
Adele Prandini

Accepts unsolicited scripts. Returns scripts with SASE. Submit full script, typed. Produces musicals and one-acts. Considers scripts that have been previously produced. Considers scripts that have been produced in workshop. Scripts must have lesbian and/or gay characters and sensibilities. Prefers scripts with maximum of 10 characters. Does not produce under any Equity contracts. Responds to script submissions in 6 months. Pays royalties.

W.O.W. CAFE

59 East 4th Street
New York, NY 10003
(212) 460-8067
Maureen Angelos

Does not accept unsolicited scripts. Does not produce under any Equity contracts. W.O.W. is a women's theater run by a loose collective of volunteers, mainly lesbian; the best way to get a show here is to live around New York and get involved in our shows. W.O.W. produces works in any genre (musical, drama, performance art) almost always generated by members of the group. Some seasons feature a cabaret, which welcomes 10-minute acts in anything, by members and non members alike.

WINGS THEATER COMPANY

154 Christopher Street
New York, NY 10014
(212) 627-2960
Fax: (212) 462-0024
E-mail: cjeffer@brainlink.com
World Wide Web:
http://www.brainlink.com/~cjeffer/
Laurie Kleeman

Accepts unsolicited scripts. Returns scripts with SASE. Submit full-length script only. Scripts should be typed. Produces musicals. Does not produce one-acts. Considers scripts that have been produced in workshop. Does not produce under any Equity contracts. Responds to script submissions each September. Pays fee of $100 or 5% of box office, whichever is greater; 5% of box office, if production is extended. Produces 2 series; Gay Play Series: musicals, comedies, and dramas with major gay characters or theme; New Musicals Series: previously unproduced musicals, no limits on content.

Agents

THE AHEARN AGENCY, INC.*
2021 Pine Street
New Orleans, LA 70118
(504) 861-8395
Fax: (504) 866-6434
E-mail: pahearn@aol.com
Pamela Ahearn

15% commission. Represents lesbian and gay writers. Interested in fiction and nonfiction. Charges reading fee. Reads unsolicited queries. Query should include SASE. Responds to queries in 4 weeks. Does not read unsolicited MSS. Returns MSS with SASE.

ALISON PICARD, LITERARY AGENT
P.O. Box 2000
Cotuit, MA 02635
(508) 477-7192
Fax: (508) 420-0762
Alison Picard

15% commission. Represents lesbian and gay writers. Interested in fiction, nonfiction, spirituality, historical, and religious subjects. Reads unsolicited queries. Query should include SASE. Responds to queries in 1 week. Does not read unsolicited MSS.

CAROLYN JENKS AGENCY*
205 Walden Street, Suite 1A
Cambridge, MA 02140-3507
(617) 876-6927

15% commission (10% for film and TV; 20% for foreign rights). Considers lesbian and gay material. Interested in fiction and trade nonfiction.

Does not read unsolicited queries. Responds to queries in 4–6 weeks. Returns MSS with SASE. Listed with *Literary Market Place, Writer's Digest,* National Writers Union, Writers Guild of America signatory. Co-sponsor of a writers' retreat in Montana. Write for brochure.

CHARLES STOUGH
2517 Rugby Road
Dayton, OH 45406-2133
(513) 278-6412
E-mail: copyboy@dma.org

10% commission. Represents straight, lesbian and gay writers. Interested in fiction, nonfiction, historical subjects, and humor. Reads unsolicited queries. Query should include SASE. Responds to queries in 1–4 weeks. Reads unsolicited MSS for a $250 reading fee. Responds to MS readings in 2–8 weeks. Returns MSS with SASE. Tips: "We expect submissions first to be high-quality writing, second to be 'gay' writing. We do not represent pornography."

CHARLOTTE GUSAY LITERARY AGENCY
10532 Blythe
Los Angeles, CA 90064
(310) 559-0831
Charlotte Gusay

15% commission on books, 10% on screenplays. Represents lesbian and gay writers. Interested in fiction and nonfiction. Reads unsolicited queries. Query should include SASE. Responds to queries in 2–6 weeks. Responds to MS submissions in 6–10 weeks. Returns MSS with SASE.

ELLEN LEVINE LITERARY AGENCY

15 East 26th Street, Suite 1801
New York, NY 10010
(212) 889-0620
Diane Finch or Louise Quayle

15% commission. Represents lesbian and gay writers. Interested in fiction, nonfiction, historical, and spiritual subjects. Reads unsolicited queries. Query should include SASE. Responds to queries in 1–2 weeks. Does not read unsolicited MSS.

THE LAZEAR AGENCY

430 1st Avenue North, Suite 416
Minneapolis, MN 55401
(612) 332-8640
Editorial Board

15% commission. Represents lesbian and gay writers. Interested in fiction, nonfiction, spirituality, and historical subjects. Reads unsolicited queries. Query should include SASE. Responds to queries in 7–10 days. Does not read unsolicited MSS. Does not return MSS.

LOWENSTEIN MOREL ASSOCIATES*

121 West 27th Street #601
New York, NY 10001
(212) 206-1630
Fax: (212) 727-0280

Interested in gay and lesbian writing. Reads unsolicited queries and MSS. Interested in fiction, nonfiction, erotica, religious, spirituality, and news subjects. Queries should include SASE. Responds to MS and query submissions in 2 weeks to 1 month.

MALAGA BALDI LITERARY AGENCY

2112 Broadway, Suite 403
New York, NY 10023
(212) 579-5075
Fax: (212) 579-5078
E-mail: mbaldi@aol.com
Malaga Baldi

15% commission. Represents lesbian and gay writers. Interested in fiction and nonfiction. Reads unsolicited queries. Query should include SASE. Minimum 10-week response reading time. Reads unsolicited MSS. Returns MSS with SASE or check to cover return via UPS.

MICHAEL LARSEN/ELIZABETH POMADA, LITERARY AGENTS

1029 Jones Street
San Francisco, CA 94109
(415) 673-0939
Michael Larsen or Elizabeth Pomada

15% commission. Reads unsolicited queries. For nonfiction, phone first. For fiction, prefers first 30 pages and synopsis. Queries should include SASE. Responds to queries in 8 weeks. Does not read unsolicited MSS. Returns MSS with SASE. Tips: "We're looking for fresh voices and new ideas, for books that are irresistible. Good writing is of primary importance. The gay angle is secondary, although this audience is wonderful."

SCOTT MEREDITH LITERARY AGENCY, L.P.

845 Third Avenue
New York, NY 10022-6687
(212) 751-4545
Fax: (212) 755-2972
Joshua Bilmes

10% commission. Represents lesbian and gay writers. Interested in fiction and nonfiction. Reads unsolicited queries. Query should include SASE. Responds to queries in 2–3 weeks. Does not read unsolicited MSS.

Subject Index

General Index

126

BOOKS FROM CLEIS PRESS

Gender Transgression

Body Alchemy: Transsexual Portraits
by Loren Cameron.
Lambda Literary Award Winner.
ISBN: 1-57344-062-0 24.95 paper.

Dagger: On Butch Women,
edited by Roxxie, Lily Burana, Linnea Due.
ISBN: 0-939416-82-4 14.95 paper.

*I Am My Own Woman: The Outlaw Life
of Charlotte von Mahlsdorf,*
translated by Jean Hollander.
ISBN: 1-57344-010-8 12.95 paper.

*PoMoSexuals: Challenging Assumptions
About Gender and Sexuality,*
edited by Carol Queen
and Lawrence Schimel.
Preface by Kate Bornstein.
ISBN: 1-57344-074-4 14.95 paper.

Sex Changes: The Politics of Transgenderism
by Pat Califia
ISBN: 1-57344-072-8 16.95 paper.

*Switch Hitters: Lesbians Write Gay Male
Erotica and Gay Men Write Lesbian Erotica,*
edited by Carol Queen
and Lawrence Schimel.
ISBN: 1-57344-021-3 12.95 paper.

Sexual Politics

*Forbidden Passages:
Writings Banned in Canada,*
introductions by Pat Califia
and Janine Fuller.
Lambda Literary Award Winner.
ISBN: 1-57344-019-1 14.95 paper.

Public Sex: The Culture of Radical Sex
by Pat Califia.
ISBN: 0-939416-89-1 12.95 paper.

*Real Live Nude Girl:
Chronicles of Sex-Positive Culture*
by Carol Queen.
ISBN: 1-57344-073-6. 14.95 paper.

*Sex Work:
Writings by Women in the Sex Industry,*
edited by Frédérique Delacoste
and Priscilla Alexander.
ISBN: 0-939416-11-5 16.95 paper.

*Susie Bright's Sexual Reality:
A Virtual Sex World Reader*
by Susie Bright.
ISBN: 0-939416-59-X 9.95 paper.

Susie Bright's Sexwise
by Susie Bright.
ISBN: 1-57344-002-7 10.95 paper.

Susie Sexpert's Lesbian Sex World
by Susie Bright.
ISBN: 0-939416-35-2 9.95 paper.

Erotic Literature
Best Gay Erotica 1998,
selected by Christopher Bram,
edited by Richard Labonté.
ISBN: 1-57344-031-0 14.95 paper.

Best Gay Erotica 1997,
selected by Douglas Sadownick,
edited by Richard Labonté.
ISBN: 1-57344-067-1 14.95 paper.

Best Gay Erotica 1996,
selected by Scott Heim,
edited by Michael Ford.
ISBN: 1-57344-052-3 12.95 paper.

Best Lesbian Erotica 1998,
selected by Jenifer Levin,
edited by Tristan Taormino.
ISBN: 1-57344-032-9 14.95 paper.

Best Lesbian Erotica 1997,
selected by Jewelle Gomez,
edited by Tristan Taormino.
ISBN: 1-57344-065-5 14.95 paper.

*Serious Pleasure: Lesbian Erotic
Stories and Poetry,*
edited by the Sheba Collective.
ISBN: 0-939416-45-X 9.95 paper.

Lesbian and Gay Studies
The Case of the Good-for-Nothing Girlfriend
by Mabel Maney.
Lambda Literary Award Nominee.
ISBN: 0-939416-91-3 10.95 paper.

The Case of the Not-So-Nice Nurse
by Mabel Maney.
Lambda Literary Award Nominee.
ISBN: 0-939416-76-X 9.95 paper.

*Nancy Clue and the Hardly Boys in
A Ghost in the Closet*
by Mabel Maney.
Lambda Literary Award Nominee.
ISBN: 1-57344-012-4 10.95 paper.

*Different Daughters:
A Book by Mothers of Lesbians,*
second edition,
edited by Louise Rafkin.
ISBN: 1-57344-050-7 12.95 paper.

*Different Mothers: Sons & Daughters of
Lesbians Talk About Their Lives,*
edited by Louise Rafkin.
Lambda Literary Award Winner.
ISBN: 0-939416-41-7 9.95 paper.

A Lesbian Love Advisor
by Celeste West.
ISBN: 0-939416-26-3 9.95 paper.

On the Rails: A Memoir,
second edition,
by Linda Niemann.
Introduction by Leslie Marmon Silko.
ISBN: 1-57344-064-7. 14.95 paper.

Queer Dog: Homo/Pup/Poetry,
edited by Gerry Gomez Pearlberg.
ISBN: 1-57344-071-X. 12.95. paper.

Sex Guides

Good Sex: Real Stories
from Real People,
second edition,
by Julia Hutton.
ISBN: 1-57344-000-0 14.95 paper.

The New Good Vibrations Guide to Sex:
Tips and Techniques from America's Favorite
Sex-toy Store, second edition,
by Cathy Winks and Anne Semans.
ISBN: 1-57344-069-8 21.95 paper.

The Ultimate Guide to Anal Sex for Women
by Tristan Taormino.
ISBN: 1-57344-028-0 14.95 paper.

Debut Fiction

Memory Mambo
by Achy Obejas.
Lambda Literary Award Winner.
ISBN: 1-57344-017-5 12.95 paper.

We Came All The Way from Cuba So You
Could Dress Like This?:
Stories by Achy Obejas.
Lambda Literary Award Nominee.
ISBN: 0-939416-93-X 10.95 paper.

Seeing Dell
by Carol Guess
ISBN: 1-57344-023-X 12.95 paper.

World Literature

A Forbidden Passion
by Cristina Peri Rossi.
ISBN: 0-939416-68-9 9.95 paper.

Half a Revolution: Contemporary Fiction by
Russian Women,
edited by Masha Gessen.
ISBN 1-57344-006-X $12.95 paper.

The Little School: Tales of Disappearance
and Survival in Argentina
by Alicia Partnoy.
ISBN: 0-939416-07-7 9.95 paper.

Peggy Deery: An Irish Family at War
by Nell McCafferty.
ISBN: 0-939416-39-5 9.95 paper.

Thrillers & Dystopias

Another Love
by Erzsébet Galgóczi.
ISBN: 0-939416-51-4 8.95 paper.

Dirty Weekend: A Novel of Revenge
by Helen Zahavi.
ISBN: 0-939416-85-9 10.95 paper.

Only Lawyers Dancing
by Jan McKemmish.
ISBN: 0-939416-69-7 9.95 paper.

The Wall
by Marlen Haushofer.
ISBN: 0-939416-54-9 9.95 paper.

Vampires & Horror

Brothers of the Night:
Gay Vampire Stories
edited by Michael Rowe
and Thomas S. Roche.
ISBN: 1-57344-025-6 14.95 paper.

Dark Angels:
Lesbian Vampire Stories,
edited by Pam Keesey.
Lambda Literary Award Nominee.
ISBN 1-7344-014-0 10.95 paper.

130

Daughters of Darkness:
Lesbian Vampire Stories,
edited by Pam Keesey.
ISBN: 0-939416-78-6 9.95 paper.

Vamps: An Illustrtated History
of the Femme Fatale
by Pam Keesey.
ISBN: 1-57344-026-4 21.95.

Sons of Darkness: Tales of Men,
Blood and Immortality,
edited by Michael Rowe
and Thomas S. Roche.
Lambda Literary Award Nominee.
ISBN: 1-57344-059-0 12.95 paper.

Women Who Run with the Werewolves: Tales
of Blood, Lust, and Metamorphosis,
edited by Pam Keesey.
Lambda Literary Award Nominee.
ISBN: 1-57344-057-4 12.95 paper.

Politics of Health
The Absence of the Dead Is Their
Way of Appearing
by Mary Winfrey Trautmann.
ISBN: 0-939416-04-2 8.95 paper.

Don't: A Woman's Word
by Elly Danica.
ISBN: 0-939416-22-0 8.95 paper

Voices in the Night:
Women Speaking About Incest,
edited by Toni A. H. McNaron
and Yarrow Morgan.
ISBN: 0-939416-02-6 9.95 paper.

With the Power of Each Breath:
A Disabled Women's Anthology,
edited by Susan Browne,
Debra Connors and Nanci Stern.
ISBN: 0-939416-06-9 10.95 paper.

Comix
Dyke Strippers: Lesbian Cartoonists A to Z,
edited by Roz Warren.
ISBN: 1-57344-008-6 16.95 paper.

The Night Audrey's Vibrator Spoke:
A Stonewall Riots Collection
by Andrea Natalie.
Lambda Literary Award Nominee.
ISBN: 0-939416-64-6 8.95 paper.

Revenge of Hothead Paisan:
Homicidal Lesbian Terrorist
by Diane DiMassa.
Lambda Literary Award Nominee.
ISBN: 1-57344-016-7 16.95 paper.

Travel & Cooking
Betty and Pansy's Severe Queer
Review of New York
by Betty Pearl and Pansy.
ISBN: 1-57344-070-1 10.95 paper.

Betty and Pansy's Severe Queer
Review of San Francisco
by Betty Pearl and Pansy.
ISBN: 1-57344-056-6 10.95 paper.

Food for Life & Other Dish,
edited by Lawrence Schimel.
ISBN: 1-57344-061-2 14.95 paper.

Writer's Reference
*Putting Out: The Essential Publishing
Resource Guide for Gay and Lesbian
Writers,* fourth edition,
by Edisol W. Dotson.
ISBN: 1-57344-033-7 14.95 paper.

Since 1980, Cleis Press has published provocative, smart books—for girlfriends of all genders. Cleis Press books are easy to find at your favorite bookstore—or direct from us! We welcome your order and will ship your books as quickly as possible. Individual orders must be prepaid (U.S. dollars only). Please add 15% shipping. CA residents add 8.5% sales tax. MasterCard and Visa orders: include account number, exp. date, and signature.

How to Order
- **Phone:** 1 (800)780-2279 or (415) 575-4700
  Monday–Friday, 9 am–5 pm Pacific Standard Time
- **Fax:** (415) 575-4705
- **Mail:** Cleis Press P.O. Box 14684, San Francisco, California 94114
- **E-mail:** Cleis@aol.com